A HISTORY OF
BOURNEMOUTH
SEAFRONT

A HISTORY OF
BOURNEMOUTH
SEAFRONT

ANDREW EMERY

*This book is dedicated to my family: Mum, Dad, Jo, Millie —
and of course Milo the dog.*

Frontispiece: Britain's All Seasons Resort: The Official Guide to
Bournemouth 1938/39.

First published in 2008 by
The History Press
The Mill, Brimscombe Port,
Stroud, Gloucestershire, GL5 2QG
www.thehistorypress.co.uk

Reprinted in 2008, 2013

British Library Cataloguing in Publication Data.
A catalogue record for this book is available from the British Library.

ISBN 978 0 7524 4717 5

Typesetting and origination by
The History Press.
Printed in Great Britain

Contents

Acknowledgements

Andrew Emery is a member of the seafront management team having worked for Bournemouth Borough Council since 2001. He studied history at York University, graduating in 1994.

The author would like to thank the following organisations and individuals who made possible the publication of this book: Bournemouth Borough Council archive, John Cresswell and the Bournemouth Natural Science Society, The Russell Cotes Art Gallery & Museum, Simon Adamson, Rachel McArdle, Jan Marsh, Joe Hart, Brian Cummings, Chris Saunders, Roger Brown, Boscombe Library, Bournemouth Library, Delia Cutler, Ray Ford, Pat Roe, John Gibbons, Mr N. Ward, Jo Mountain, Marriott Highcliff Hotel, Bournemouth Tourism, Mrs Chave.

Introduction

Bournemouth's seafront has embraced generations of visitors over the past 180 years, developing an unrivalled reputation for outstanding natural beauty, glorious golden sands and simple seaside pleasures. Never quite the cosmopolitan rival to Brighton or the cheeky, eager to please equal of Blackpool, Bournemouth has nevertheless carved a reputation as one of the 'big three' seaside resorts, frequently winning the accolade 'Britain's best beach'. And unlike the other two, a rising line of cliffs dramatically separates Bournemouth's beach from the hustle and bustle of the town behind.

Geography dictates that there's little room for the roller coasters and pleasure palaces that entertain and amuse visitors at other beach resorts. Bournemouth's beach is left to weave its own special magic over millions of visitors every year without recourse to flashy gimmicks and distractions. Its story, the story of how it came to captivate a nation of holidaymakers, has rarely been told. It is a story that reveals our enduring pleasures and our vaunting ambitions. There's vanity and more than a little greed along the road to staggering success. It's often been said that life is at its most revealing on the margins; in this case, where the land ends and the sea begins.

I came to work at the seafront in 2004 and my first few months were spent just trying to survive a very busy summer. It wasn't until that winter that I had my first opportunity to consider the history of the seafront. There were a few old timers who knew some of the stories – real characters with sun-creased faces. One of them came into my office during a storm, dripping water over the papers on my desk. 'Get your coat and I'll show you an old secret about this place,' he said. We

Above: Deck games – 'a novel attraction which entertains crowds of visitors on Bournemouth Pier', 1930. (Leisure Services)

Left: Punch and Judy on the beach – a firm favourite in 1935 and occasionally still to be seen today. (Bournemouth Tourism)

Opposite: Bournemouth Pier from the air in 1928. The promenade between the West Cliff Lift and Durley Chine is under construction in this picture. (Leisure Services)

went outside onto the rain-lashed promenade. The waves were scouring out the beach, revealing black streaks of hard sand. We walked down to the beach next to the promenade and my colleague reached down into the crevices between stone blocks at the lower reaches of the sea wall. After a while he pulled out an old coin. He brushed it on his coat and rubbed it with his finger then handed it to me with a smile. The coin was badly worn but you could make out it was an Edward VII halfpenny from the early 1900s. 'You'll find plenty more,' he winked, pulling out a handful of Edwardian loose change. I pictured visitors losing their change on the beach 100 years ago in just the same way as dozens of car keys and mobile phones are lost in the sand today. I imagined countless people year after year, standing on the same spot and admiring the naturally framed view with the Isle of Purbeck to the west and Hengistbury Head and the Isle of Wight to the east. I wondered what had changed over the years and what had remained the same.

one

Discovering
the View

Alum Chine Beach looking towards Bournemouth, in the early 1900s, long before the promenade was built. This is a beach scene the author Robert Louis Stevenson would have been familiar with. He lived in a house, Skerryvore, at the top of the Chine between 1885-1887, where he wrote *Kidnapped* and *Strange Case of Dr. Jekyll and Mr. Hyde*. (Undated postcard: Bournemouth Libraries)

Smugglers at Bourne Mouth, from a painting by Henry Perlee Parker (1795–1873). The central figure is supposed to represent Isaac Gulliver the most famous of local smugglers, who died at Wimborne in 1822. (Bournemouth Libraries)

From left to right: Robert Lever, chief collector, Boscombe Pier; W.C. Knottley, assistant pier master, Bournemouth Pier; Captain W. Neuman, pier master, Bournemouth Pier; E. Baskett, assistant pier master Boscombe., 1907. By tradition, the pier masters were usually retired naval officers. (*Bournemouth Graphic*)

Unlike the majority of English seaside resorts Bournemouth did not expand out of an established fishing village or existing community. It was purpose built as a resort out of little more than heathland scrub which had been extensively planted with Scotch and Pinaster fir after the passing of the Christchurch Enclosure Act in 1802.

A chalk coastline had once stretched unbroken between the Isle of Purbeck and the Isle of Wight. Once this was breached 15,000 years ago, the coast quickly retreated to form Poole Bay. People had made a living from this stretch of coastline for thousands of years. Nearby Hengistbury Head had been a significant Iron Age settlement and a key trading port with continental Europe. Work in 1969 to shore-up the east cliff top near the Carlton Hotel revealed the remains of an Iron Age dwelling and it is certain that small communities would have lived off the abundant fishing grounds all along the Bournemouth coast. The archaeology suggests that most of these early settlements were abandoned in the fifth century AD as the Roman legions left, exposing the coastline to piracy and invasion.

The Bournemouth coast remained largely un-populated into the sixteenth century when the Earl of Southampton's coastal defence plans drawn up in 1574 against an expected Spanish invasion showed little habitation in the area. Ten years earlier, in 1564, Lord Mountjoy had secured a monopoly licence from Queen Elizabeth I to mine for alum and copperas, minerals used in the leather tanning and paper industries. Extensive travels in Europe had taught Mountjoy to read the landscape and uncover rich mineral deposits. Local folklore has it that when passing

Lewis Tregonwell (1758-1832) founder resident of Bournemouth. Taken from a portrait painted by Thomas Bench in 1798. Tregonwell wears the uniform of a captain in the Dorset Yeomanry and in this capacity was stationed along the Bournemouth coast in the 1790s. (Bournemouth Libraries)

through the neighbourhood he noticed an abundance of naturally occurring holly bushes around the tops of what are today Middle Chine and Alum Chine. This was a sign that deposits might be found and his mine workings gave Alum Chine its name. Chine or 'Cinn' was the Old English name for a small wooded valley. Unfortunately, Lord Mountjoy's monopoly claims were disputed in court and he was bankrupted by litigation. However, a map of 1647 still recorded an Allom house perched on the cliff top above.

By the eighteenth century high taxation on imported goods was imposed to pay for England's continental wars and this inadvertently encouraged illegal smuggling

Lewis Tregonwell's mansion house was built in 1811 to overlook the mouth of the River Bourne and the sweeping sands of the bay. It was the first property in the area devoted to the pleasure and enjoyment of the seaside. The building now forms part of the Royal Exeter Hotel. (Bournemouth Libraries)

Benjamin Ferry was commissioned by the Gervis estate to devise a plan for the town. This particular vision, dated 1836, was never fully executed, but illustrates the desire to build a pier right from the start. (Bournemouth Libraries)

of luxury goods such as liquor, sugar and tea all along the south coast. The isolated cliffs and coves around present-day Bournemouth became a popular smugglers' haunt. A network of paths led from the coast to cottages and inns with trap doors and secret cellars. Whole communities would be complicit with the trade which frequently involved dozens of men rowing out at night to cargo ships moored in the bay.

The government established a coastguard station on the rising cliff top to the west of the Bourne Valley in an attempt to combat this illicit trade. This building survives as part of an annex of fifteen deluxe bedrooms within the grounds of the Marriott Highcliff Hotel adjacent to the Bournemouth International Centre.

The coastguard men referred to the small depressions in the cliffs as Chines. The present-day Beacon steps leading down from the BIC was known as Rickes Chine while the West Cliff Zig-Zag was named Watery Chine.

The most notable local smuggler was an inn keeper called Isaac Gulliver. Born in 1745 he spent a lifetime smuggling on an almost industrial scale and never once got caught. His band of up to fifty smugglers cocked a snook at symbols of authority by wearing gentlemen's powdered wigs and were known collectively as the 'white wigs'. By the time of his last smuggling run in 1800 he had three fully laden luggers anchored off the beach and a two-mile-long convoy of horse and wagons tramping its way across the heath towards the village of Kinson, now a suburb of Bournemouth. Gulliver supposedly rode a white horse at the head of this cavalcade.

The rise of the Romantic Movement at the beginning of the nineteenth century slowly began to change people's perceptions of a lawless and dangerous coastline. Britain's mastery of the seas during the Napoleonic Wars brought security from invasion for the first time since Romano-Britain, paving the way for genteel habitation as wealthy people sought to live amidst the wild and rugged scenery.

Lewis Tregonwell, a Dorset landowner born in 1758 had been stationed in the area in 1797 at the head of a troop of horse militia to guard against a possible French invasion. Some years later he brought his wife Henrietta to the nearby village of Mudeford to help her recover from a deep depression following the death of their three-year-old son, who had been given an accidental overdose of medicine to sooth a fit of fretfulness.

They engaged in the new fashion for sea bathing and on 14 June they took a carriage drive over the heathland towards the mouth of the Bourne stream to view the area he had once patrolled. Henrietta cheerfully suggested that this would be the perfect place to build a holiday home. Tregonwell duly purchased eight acres from Sir George Tapps for £179 11s and built a home overlooking the sea, which today forms part of the Royal Exeter Hotel. They moved in with a new baby son, called John, in 1812.

Over the next few years he purchased more land to build a few cottages and also took ownership of the nearby Tapps Arms, known locally as a smugglers' inn. By the early 1820s the Tregonwell's had moved back to their main residence at Cranborne Lodge and were renting out the Mansion, as their holiday home was affectionately called, to a series of tenants who came to enjoy the seclusion and sea views.

One early visitor, a Mrs Arbuthnott, wrote in 1824:

I rode one day to a place called Bournemouth – a collection of hills lately planted by a gentleman of the name of Tregonwell who had built four or five beautiful cottages which he lets out to persons who go sea-bathing. I was so charmed with the beauty of the situation that Mr. Arbuthnott and myself agreed to take one next summer for the sake of a little sea-bathing.

There was little further development over the next ten years and the beach remained a secluded retreat for persons of quality such as the Marchioness of Exeter, who rented the Mansion in the 1830s. The wild fir woods and heathland surrounding the area was chiefly used for shooting game, specifically hen harrier, by the Earl of Malmesbury, who owned land adjacent to Sir George Tapps.

When Sir George died, his son, George William Tapps-Gervis invited the architect Benjamin Ferry in 1836 to layout a design for a resort consisting of luxury villas spaced out along the eastern side of the Bourne Valley. Ferry's vision was for a high class resort with a seaside pier at the mouth of the Bourne stream. The pier was not built at the time but on Queen Victoria's coronation day on 28 June 1838 the Bath Hotel opened, and a further hotel called the Belle Vue boarding house opened in 1841 on the site of what is now the Pavilion. In addition, a small public sea-water baths was built near the beach on the site of the present-day Waterfront building around 1840. This establishment, run by Alfred Roberts, also offered use of bathing machines on the beach. By 1842 an exclusive marine village had evolved consisting of less than forty buildings and a population of around 250 people.

two

Bournemouth Gets
a Health Kick

The early development of Britain's seaside resorts owes much to the popularisation of seawater bathing by the medical profession. As a direct result, a visit to the seaside became fashionable amongst the upper classes from the 1750s onwards. There is plenty of evidence to suggest that sea bathing and drinking seawater for health-tonic reasons was being advocated and practiced in this country as far back as the sixteenth century. One publication noted in 1581 that, 'the swimming in salt water is very good to remove the headache, to open the suffed nosethilles, and thereby to helpe the smelling. It is a good remedie for dropsies, scabbes and scurfes, small pockes, leprosies, falling away of either legge, or any other parte.'

The Tregonwells were great fans of sea bathing first at Mudeford and later at Bournemouth. Sea bathing in the eighteenth and early nineteenth did not mean swimming. Few people knew how to swim; indeed modern swimming strokes had not even been invented. The practice of sea bathing involved being immersed or 'dipped' into the sea, usually with the help of an attendant or 'dipper'. The seafront's first piece of iconic architecture, the bathing machine, was devised in the eighteenth century to afford persons of quality some modesty and protection from prying eyes as they negotiated their way into the water. The prospective bather would wait for a machine to be drawn up the beach, usually by pony. He or she would enter the machine and dress down to a simple gown while the attendant wheeled them into the shallows. They would then help the bather down steps and into the water for perhaps half a dozen short spells before driving them back up the beach. The process was highly ritualised and would probably be followed by further ablutions inside the public baths.

First mention of bathing machines in Bournemouth dates back to 1826 in connection with Tregonwell's Mansion. By 1831 there were at least three bathing machines available for hire. By 1874 the beach was 'amply provided for by a goodly number of bathing machines' located between the East Cliff Zig-Zag, or Steps Chine as it was then known, and Joseph Steps, or the West Cliff Zig-Zag today. Alfred Roberts operated the machines at Bournemouth and a Mr Cutler ran further machines for hire at Durley Chine.

The cure-all claims of sea bathing continued in publications like Dr A.B. Granville's *The Spas of England* which staked a claim for the as yet 'unformed colony' of Bournemouth as 'a perfect discovery among the sea-nooks one longs to have for a real invalid.' At this time Bournemouth was still largely unknown even to the regular patrons of nearby Weymouth, a resort which had been popular for decades.

These bathing machines were operated by an attendant based in the small hut in the middle of the picture. A pony is on hand to help drag the machines into and out of the water, *c.* 1865. (Bournemouth Libraries)

Dr Granville's first volume of *The Spas of England* had been published to great acclaim and so the early residents of Bournemouth had invited him to a public dinner at the Bath Hotel in 1841. Suitably impressed, he wrote a glowing account of his visit, concluding, 'that no situation . . . along the whole southern coast possesses so many capabilities of being made the very first invalid sea-watering place in England.'

Granville praised the:

. . . Balsamic and almost medicinal emanations from fir plantations . . . gentle curvilinear sweep of coast composed of 'fine white sand . . . Here and there, among the topping white sands, white pipeclay has been found, but neither continuously nor in thick masses, except near the cliff to the east of Boscomb, and at Big Durley-chine, where it is worked out and sent to the potteries in Staffordshire . . . The cliffs vary occasionally in height, but except where a chine or valley occurs to interrupt the continuous line their elevation is seldom less than sixty, and often exceeds 150 feet. Of these chines . . . there are several. Some are mere indentures in the sand beds, more or less profound, due to the percolation of water digging into the sand; others are real valleys. Bournemouth is just one of these valley chines. At the foot of the cliff is the shore, covered with the usual shingle, being

Engraving entitled *South East view of Bournemouth* by H. Daniel, *c.*1845. (Bournemouth Libraries)

Boscombe Chine from the beach, *c.*1870s. The Chine spa waters can be seen trickling onto the beach and could be sampled for their health-giving properties from the thatched shelter. The Boscombe Chine Hotel sits on the cliff top above. (Bournemouth Libraries)

part of the coarse, moderately-sized gravel noticed in the strata . . . at the lower part of the cliff. Between the foot of the cliff and the bed of sea-shingle, there are in many parts of the strand wide and extended belts of sand, which at high tide offer an excellent footing to the bather. Westward of Bournemouth there are other interruptions or chines in the cliffs, such as Little Durly, Big Durly, Broad, Middle and Alum Chine.

Dr Granville was also the first to popularise the notion that Bournemouth was ideally suited all year round for invalids owing to its mild climate. This idea was continuously reflected in publicity material well into the twentieth century with slogans such as 'Bournemouth: where summer winters' taken from 1950s tourist brochures. Dr Granville extolled the pure sea air, sea-water bathing and the inspiring landscape, ideal for exercise on horseback, but he also cautioned against over-development which might spoil the natural prospect of the landscape. Like Benjamin Ferry before him, Dr Granville did recommend the creation of a short pier and a cove to 'admit a few pleasure boats.'

The second volume of Dr Granville's *The Spas of England* had a profound effect on the growth of the town and the seafront. In 1855 a national sanatorium for consumption and diseases of the chest was founded in Bournemouth. Patients could stay, upon production of a medical certificate and nomination from the governor, for 6s per week. The following year the town had reached sufficient size to warrant an Improvement Act of Parliament and the creation of a body of elected Improvement Commissioners to oversee the provision of drainage, paving and amenities to the growing town.

By 1860, Dr Spencer Thompson was describing Bournemouth as the 'winter garden of England.' He noted two types of invalid inhabiting and visiting the town. Many had arrived after years of service in hot climates abroad to recover their constitutions and gently acclimatise to the 'cold and dampness which prevail over by far the greater part of Great Britain.' There were also the young who had weak and delicate constitutions.

Having fun, however, was not so high on the agenda for the new resort. The author of Sydenham's *Illustrated Guide to Bournemouth* recalled early visits in the 1850s as terribly dull:

I was compelled to endure more than one mild picnic with Anglican spinsters in Boscombe Chine . . . and in the days before piers, or bathing establishments or restaurants were born or thought of, I have helped,

Engraving entitled *The sands, Bournemouth by P. Brannon*, 1855. (Bournemouth Libraries)

with a dozen men – the sole available maritime population of Bournemouth – to float an old collier, which had been blown high and dry on the sands in a storm, and it took three good weeks to do it.

The 1860s also saw the seafront develop as a mecca for amateur naturalists and photographers. The first attempts at understanding and classifying the natural topography, plant and animal life date from this time. Not everyone saw value in the local flora and fauna, though. The author of *The Origin of Species*, Charles Darwin, came to stay in 1862 whilst one of his children recovered from scarlet fever. He wrote to his friend John Lubbock, 'I do nothing here except occasionally look at a few flowers, and there are very few here, for the country is wonderfully barren.'

three

We Have Arrived!

Prior to the arrival of the railway in Bournemouth in 1870, the quickest and cheapest way to travel round the country was by sea and many of the first seaside resorts owed their success to possessing a harbour or port. Bournemouth had no facility to receive visitors by sea. A pier, Dr Granville claimed back in 1841, was 'very essential to those who are desirous of water excursions', it being 'impracticable to approach the shore from a boat without being swamped, and at other times it is very difficult to get into a boat without being annoyed by the surf.'

On 3 December 1847 a meeting was held at the Bath Hotel to discuss the formation of a private company to raise the necessary finance to build a pier. The money was not easily forthcoming and so the first pier was a very modest affair, little more than a jetty or landing stage 6ft wide and 100ft long. It was located adjacent to the position of the present-day Bournemouth Pier on the east side and was built by Samuel Ingram between 1855-56. Opened to great acclaim on 20 August 1856 it swiftly succumbed to storm damage, and despite repeated repairs was largely dismantled in 1861. At least fourteen of the tightly spaced wooden support piles remained protruding from the sand close to the waterline for some years as a reminder of its failure.

The Bournemouth Improvement Act of 1856 created the first official governing body for the town in the form of elected commissioners. One of their primary tasks outlined in section III of the Act was for them to build a pier within five years. The Act also empowered the commissioners to levy a toll on persons and merchandise landing or embarking from the pier. A detailed schedule of charges was appended to the Act.

In this way the creation and maintenance of a pier was fundamental to the establishment of a body which would eventually become the local council. The pier was the first public project designed to galvanise the economic development of the town.

On behalf of the town the commissioners purchased a freehold interest of land from the Meyrick Estate and consulting engineer George Rennie was hired to design a new wooden pier. He submitted a plan for a 1,000ft-long pier, 15ft wide and built of softwood timber. The contract to build the structure was entrusted to David Thornbury, an engineer on holiday from Newcastle-on-Tyne. He boasted that it would be a 'trifling occupation to knock off the pier.' His tender for £3,418 was accepted with alacrity and the first timber piles were driven into the beach alongside the remains of the jetty on 25 July 1859.

The occasion was marked by festivities but the optimistic mood soon ebbed when a severe gale a few weeks later swept everything away. Work had to start again

An engraved view of the seafront, as if approaching Bournemouth Pier by steamer. (*Bournemouth Directory 1887*)

Bournemouth from the water, an engraving by R. Sydenham, showing the jetty. (Bournemouth Libraries)

from scratch before grinding to a halt whilst disputes between the designer and the contractor were ironed out. Then, embarrassingly for the commissioners, the bank in which they lodged all the funds for the works failed.

The pier was finally completed and opened by Sir George Gervis on 17 September 1861. The town staged a grand procession through decorative triumphal arches. A country fair was held while a fireworks display and twenty-one-gun salute took place over the pier. Lady Gervis christened the pier with a bottle of wine and the *Ursa Major* steamship alighted from Poole laden with passengers and accompanying

The boy in this picture stands on the remains of the jetty in 1865, which had been replaced by the first pier four years earlier. The jetty stood just east of the pier. (Bournemouth Libraries)

An early view of the beach looking from Bournemouth Pier, 1863. The piles on which the jetty was constructed can be seen to the left of the picture. (Bournemouth Libraries)

Pier Approach from the west side in 1860. The building material in the foreground is for the first pier, then in the process of construction. The original baths, built in 1840, can be seen on the right. (Bournemouth Libraries)

brass band. The *Prince* steam yacht also hove in carrying 'a numerous and respectable party' from Weymouth.

The entrance to the pier featured a toll booth manned by a collector who was paid 12s per week and given an annual clothing allowance of two suits and two hats. A toll of 1d was levied; however a resident's season ticket could be purchased for between 5s and one guinea depending on the rateable value of their property. The toll collector did not endear himself to visitors who complained about the 'stench' emanating from his toll house and 'the nuisance occasioned by the practice of bird stuffing.'

The pier was scarcely more fortunate than its predecessor with repairs needed within six months of opening due to storm damage. Bills for the general maintenance of the pier were never ending. A note in the Bournemouth commissioners' accounts shows, for instance, than in 1864 £3 13s 6d was paid to 'Mr Bridge for beer to men tarring the Pier.' Other outgoings included painting, the provision of seats and gas lamps and treatment for the wood-boring torredo worm which seriously weakened the piles. In 1866 the wooden piles were gradually replaced with cast-iron ones from the seaward end.

Bournemouth Pier entrance and Pier Approach, *c.* 1865. (Bournemouth Libraries)

Bournemouth's first pier, early 1870s. The storm-lash spindly structure was gradually swept away. The building under construction in the foreground was a refreshment café and sits on the site of the current Harry Ramsden's fish and chip restaurant. (Bournemouth Libraries)

Engraving of the West Cliff steps in 1887. These rickety wooden steps were made from salvage washed ashore from the wreck of the first Bournemouth Pier. (*Bournemouth Illustrated*)

On 5 January 1867 further storms in the bay broke up much of the pier including the T-shaped end. The timbers washed ashore and were used to create rudimentary access steps down from the cliffs to the beach and whilst extensive repairs were carried out on the pier, the structure was now 300ft shorter in length.

Despite these setbacks the first regular sailings from Bournemouth Pier began on 1 May 1871 with the paddle steamer *Heather Belle* offering twice daily excursions to Poole and Swanage. Operated by Swanage-based owner George Burt, the *Heather Belle* occasionally undertook sailings to the Isle of Wight and Portsmouth. The service ran for six years between the months of May and October. These sailings proved immensely popular to visitors and the ever burgeoning local population. For example, on 29 June 1871 over 400 children from Bournemouth's schools of St Peters, St Clement's, St Michael's and St John's were taken on trips to Studland and Old Harry Rocks.

The pier also became a popular place to simply promenade and take in the sea breezes. Children used to fish from the end of the pier, catching smelts and whiting. Fishing became a big draw during the mackerel and herring seasons with fishermen lined out along the strand on moonlit evenings capturing the 'enormous shoals which annually visit the coast' according Butcher & Cole's guide of 1874. The guide

The first Bournemouth Pier in 1872. The *Heather Belle* is seen leaving for Swanage. Gas lighting was installed on the pier the following year. (Bournemouth Libraries)

A view from Bournemouth Pier in the early 1870s. The small shelters along the pier afforded little protection in bad weather. (Bournemouth Libraries)

Sydenham's Marine Library and reading rooms in 1865, not long after construction. The earlier baths were located at the rear of this building and offered a broad range of sea-water treatments. The building was demolished in 1934 to make way for the Pier Approach Baths in 1937. (Bournemouth Library)

went on to describe the fossilised remains of a now submerged ancient forest at the mouth of the Bourne Valley, which could be seen at low tide west of the pier. In the spring of 1871 the remains of over thirty trees in the shallows were identified as common fir or *Pinus Sylvestris*, leading to a conclusion that in prehistoric times a forest stretched far out into the bay. This underwater forest can still be found today, diving off Bournemouth Pier.

It is also claimed that the game of water polo was invented off Bournemouth Pier in 1876.

The final sailing of the *Heather Belle* took place on Saturday 7 October 1876 and the following month gales destroyed a further 100ft off the end of the pier making it too short for use by steamboats. Burt withdrew the *Heather Belle* from service as it required a new boiler after six years of hard sailing. A temporary landing stage was erected on the remaining piles from the original 1856 jetty to enable sailings for the 1877 season while the future of the pier was debated.

Burt's agent, David Sydenham, owner of Sydenham's Marine Reading Library and gift shop located in front of the baths in Pier Approach, realised the potential

Bournemouth Pier entrance building of 1880 showing the Pier Master's Office on the first floor below the clock tower. The building rattled like a green house during storms – glass breaking everywhere. This picture was taken in 1930 just prior to being demolished. (Leisure Services)

for further steamer services and contacted Weymouth-based Captain Joseph Cosens who ran a steamer service there. Various offers were put on the table and eventually a consortium called the Bournemouth Steam Packet Co. Ltd was formed. They chartered the steamer *Criterion* from Sunderland and began offering sailings on 12 July 1877. In August they announced that their:

> New fast and powerful steam vessel Criterion will, weather and other circumstances permitting, make an excursion to Cherbourg leaving Bournemouth punctually at 9am, calling at Swanage at 9.45am, returning from Cherbourg on Monday 21st at 2pm. Fare – twenty shillings.

Twenty-nine passengers hopped aboard and witnessed on the return journey a review of the French fleet firing salutes and manning the yards. The vessel battered rough seas, arriving back at Bournemouth almost nine hours later than scheduled at 10.45 p.m.

The Bournemouth commissioners and engineers responsible for building the 1878 Bournemouth Pier, taken on 15 January 1886.

The need for a new pier to replace the temporary landing stage was pressing but many local ratepayers were opposed to shouldering the expense. With the Improvement Commissioners dithering over what to do next, a private company was formed to take over the function of building and maintaining the pier. The Promenade Pier Co. did succeed in obtaining permission from the Board of Trade to build a pier costing £17,000 on condition that they secured the commissioners' interest in the remains of the existing pier. A financial agreement was never reached.

Finally, the commissioners pressed ahead with their own scheme for a new pier estimated to cost £20,000 and Parliamentary authority was obtained for work to commence in 1878. The new pier would be made of solid cast iron and the most experienced pier designer of the Victorian age was recruited.

Eugenius Birch is famous for building many pleasure piers not least of which the exuberant Brighton West Pier, now sadly lost. By 1878 he was aged sixty and fast approaching the end of his career but he quickly seized on the potential for the resort, designing not only a pier but an Undercliff Promenade, an aquarium and a swimming baths. In the event there was money only for the pier and the other schemes would have to wait – in the case of the aquarium, over 120 years!

Birch's pier design was conservative by the standards of Brighton West Pier. There would be no exotic embellishments or oriental inspired pagodas. The new Bournemouth Pier would be solidly built and simple to behold. An imposing and sober Victorian gothic glasshouse was erected at the entrance to the pier and featured separate cloak and waiting rooms for ladies and gentlemen.

The new pier was 755ft long and consisted of a neck 465ft long and 35ft wide and a wider pier head 290ft long and 110ft wide. Construction was undertaken by Bergheim & Co. of London and cost £21,600. The cast-iron piles were fitted with screw thread ends buried deep into the seabed to withstand the stormy weather and the deck was made of hard wearing pitch-pine timber from Scandinavia. Decorative cast-iron seating was arranged along each side of the pier neck and a central windbreak screen was erected down the centre of the pier head. Landing stages were built either side of the pier head out of Greenheart timbers with large cast-iron gratings providing the decking. These landing stages, replaced with new timber over time, remain the only original design feature left on Bournemouth Pier today. A small handful of old cast-iron screw-pile fittings from replaced landing stage piles still lie in the depot storage yard at Durley Chine.

The new pier was formally opened on 11 August 1880 by Sir Francis Wyatt Truscott, the Lord Mayor of London who described Bournemouth as 'the garden city of the south.' The new pier proved immediately popular as a place to promenade along. The *Bournemouth Illustrated Guide* of 1887 remarked:

During the whole of the summer months the Pier is a very favourite place of resort from nine o'clock in the morning till ten at night. It is generally well filled with persons of all ages and belonging to all ranks of society. Invalids and others to a great extent avail themselves of the sheltered seats during the day and the arrival and departure of the steamboats is also a great source of attraction to visitors generally. The Promenade Concerts of last season were greatly admired, and drew to the place every evening an immense concourse of people.

Bournemouth now had its landmark visitor attraction and had truly arrived as a modern Victorian seaside resort.

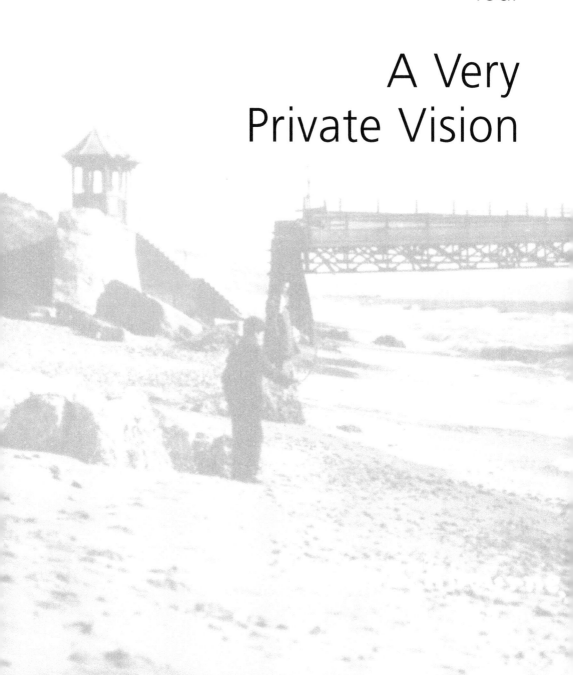

four

A Very
Private Vision

As Bournemouth began to grow in popularity during the mid-nineteenth century, local visionaries cast their eyes further along the undeveloped coast with dreams of creating rival resorts. The idea of building a dedicated health resort on barren heathland at Southbourne was taken up by a local doctor well versed in the curative value of the seaside.

Dr Thomas Armetriding Compton had been born in Sussex and qualified in medicine at Dublin in 1859. He later took up practice in Bournemouth and established a thriving private business treating wealthy patients. His spare time was spent taking regular walks across 'the Guns', as Southbourne's windswept heath was known since the coastguard practiced gunnery there. Compton quickly realised the potential for the site and the huge profits to be made from property speculation. In 1870 he raised £3,000 and purchased 230 acres of land which included 1 mile of seafront, and began setting out his vision for the resort of Southbourne-on-Sea.

Compton set up a series of limited companies to raise finance to build the infrastructure for the resort, starting with roads and bridges to connect the area with nearby Christchurch. He had the South Cliff Hotel built in 1874 and by the late 1870s private properties were springing up across the area.

In 1885 Compton built a section of sea wall with an Undercliff Promenade mounted on top and extending one third of a mile. This was the first section of seafront promenade to be built anywhere along the bay. On top of the prom he constructed a row of six stately town houses looking directly out to sea. Taking up residence in one of them himself, he offered the others out as high-class seasonal villas for wealthy patients. The plan was to create a crescent of properties all along the Undercliff Promenade. A guidebook of 1891 emphasised the unique climate of Southbourne where 'the air is pure and bracing, the temperature enviable: cold in summer and mild in winter'. A 400ft-long Winter Garden's glass house was also established on the cliff top, boasting tropical and exotic plants. Beach tents and Trouville bathing boxes, copied after a style found in the French resort, were made available to hire at 6d for the season in 1886.

The final key feature to be built was a short pier. A meeting at the South Cliff Hotel on the night of 6 November 1885 launched a public subscription towards the building of a pier at Southbourne. Numerous offers of support were given by local residents and businessmen with over £300 being raised on the night. Further shares were later issued and Compton engaged a local Southbourne man, Archibald Smith, to design the pier. E. Howell of the Waterloo foundry in Poole was employed

Engraving of the Southbourne-on-Sea Winter Gardens, 1887. (*Bournemouth Illustrated*)

to build the cast-iron structure at a cost of £4,000. The pier was quickly built and opened on 2 August 1888. The pier was simple and functional; barely 300ft long and 30ft wide, it featured a lower landing stage running across the end and two toll houses at the entrance. No seats or amusements were provided. On the first day of opening, the steamer *Lord Elgin* docked with passengers from Bournemouth and regular sailings were quickly established, including excursions to the Isle of Wight. Dr Compton must have felt confident for the future of his resort.

A sign of things to come occurred around Christmas 1898. On 27 December the *Marie Therese*, a three-masted barquentine from Le Harve, was spotted by the Southbourne coastguard close to the pier and struggling in a fierce south-westerly gale. The storm-battered promenade filled with on-lookers as they watched the vessel battle against the surging waves and avoid being driven onto the beach. Eventually, the *Marie Therese* broke up on the Beer Pan Rocks off the beach at Hengistbury Head. The newspaper reported:

Chief Officer Norkett [of the Coastguard] with many willing helpers had got the rocket apparatus out and set up near the ill-fated ship. Three rockets were fired, the last of which secured and after some little difficulty arising from some unforeseen hitches. The crew of a dozen all told (including an apprentice) were safely landed at the base of the cliffs at Warren Head to great public acclaim and cheering. It was a most rousing experience to see these men being hauled from the angry sea . . . The captain was understood to state that they had drifted up with

Southbourne Pier in 1890. Designed by local man Archibald Smith, the iron pier was a simple unadorned affair with a landing stage for steamers along the end. (Bournemouth Libraries)

Southbourne-on-Sea in 1898. Storms have wrecked the sea wall and promenade. Dr Compton's vision for an elegant crescent of town houses stretching a third of a mile was never fully realised. Only one small block was built and had been abandoned by the time of this photograph. (Bournemouth Libraries)

Storms lash Southbourne Pier in 1898, wrecking the sea wall. (Bournemouth Libraries)

Southbourne Pier was never repaired and remained in this perilous state until it was finally demolished in 1907. (Bournemouth Libraries)

the gale under close reefed sails and he had somehow missed his reckoning in making for the Solent ... The *Marie Thérèse* had its back broken and is likely to be a total wreck. She is quite close to the shore and at low water is almost accessible.

This incident served to illustrate just how angry this part of the bay could be. Coastal erosion at Southbourne had been a big problem and remains so to this day. The sea wall and promenade had been built to defend the coast and protect Compton's investment in land for without it he was loosing over 3ft of land a year. However, this prevented the natural replenishment of the beach in front of the sea wall from the previously eroding cliffs behind. Within a few short years the beach was washed away, exposing the sea wall to a pounding from the waves. The grand villas Compton had built on the promenade had to be abandoned as the waves came crashing through their front doors. Dr Compton's plan to build a long avenue of seafront villas stretching towards Hengistbury Head was in tatters. And then, bad luck played its hand.

On 28 December 1899 and 3 January 1900 further storms smashed some of the cast-iron pilings holding up the pier and breached through the sea wall. The promenade collapsed and so did one side of the landward end of the pier. The promenade houses were declared unsafe and demolished in 1902 and the remains of the prom and pier were offered to Bournemouth Council who quickly said no.

The wreckage of Compton's dreams offered a playground of unimaginable delights for local children. Mr T.A. Scott recalled in the 1950s playing as a child on the wrecked Southbourne Pier in 1906:

I used to spend much time climbing up the slope and running to the end. Then later the other shoreward support fell down making an even slope to ground level. At the shoreward end of the pier there was a flight of concrete steps leading down from the old sea wall. They stood longer than the rest and we used to refer to them as Canute's chair.

Another resident, Horace Meadowcroft, also recalled clambering over the remains of Southbourne pier as a boy: 'The sea had also made caves for local children to play pirates in. These were formed from the cellars of a hotel [the promenade houses] which once stood near the pier.'

The remains of the pier were left to rust for a handful of years before finally being demolished and removed in 1907. On 9 August that year, Dr Compton sold his interest in the Southbourne-on-Sea Freehold Land Co. and walked away.

five

A Spa is Born

Boscombe has a long tradition of striking out to rival Bournemouth at its own game. The original 'village of Boscombe Spa' was proposed back in the 1860s when the area was little more than 'a scene of indescribable desolation', according to one traveller. There were a few isolated dwellings here and there, and a chine or valley of gorse grass and sand dunes tumbling down towards the shoreline. Possessed of an undeniable picturesque wild beauty, what really secured Boscombe's future was the exploitation of a natural spring at the base of the chine.

Today, this spot is marked by a modern interpretation of the original thatched rustic summerhouse which once stood over the spring at the entrance to Boscombe Chine.

An early map of 1791 clearly marks out Boscombe Chine, with the present-day site of the gardens at the top labelled Boscombe Bottom. Aside from a few cottages and an inn called the 'Ragged Cat' Boscombe remained little more than empty heath land well into the middle of the nineteenth century.

One of the first residents to build a substantial property in the area was Sir Percy Shelley, whose father was the poet Percy Bysshe Shelley. Sir Percy enlarged an existing farm house in 1850 to create Boscombe Manor. He bought the property

Children's pony rides, Boscombe Beach, 1935. (Bournemouth Tourism)

Engraving of Shelley Chine, later known as Honeycombe Chine, 1887. (*Bournemouth Guide*)

as a summer retreat for his mother, the author Mary Shelley, but she died in 1851 before conversion work was completed. Sir Percy had his mother's remains buried in nearby St Peter's churchyard in Bournemouth and took up residence in the new house at Boscombe, building a theatre within it and devising plays and entertainments for his circle of friends.

Local land owners, the Malmesbury Estate, proposed a scheme for the 'picturesque village of Boscombe Spa' in 1866 to sell off plots of land at Boscombe on long leases and develop a settlement of marine villas as Bournemouth had done thirty years previously. But this scheme never came to fruition. Instead, Sir Henry Drummond Wolff purchased 19 acres of land in 1868 to the east of Bournemouth Chine and built a grand house called Boscombe Towers. He set about developing the area himself with the support of his neighbour Sir Percy. Sir Henry had travelled widely overseas before settling locally to become a MP for the area. The prospect of profit to be made by creating a seaside resort to imitate and perhaps even rival nearby Bournemouth was seized upon with enthusiasm by Sir Henry. The chalybeate spring water flowing down Boscombe Chine and out onto the beach had been recommended to drink for its purity and health giving properties. Sir Henry encouraged its popularity by building a small summerhouse over the spring water outfall at the bottom of the Chine. He also laid out a pathway down the Chine, a rustic wooden bridge at the top and built the Boscombe Chine Hotel in 1876 which still stands on the cliff top over the gardens. The area quickly developed into a fashionable meeting place and a perfect location for visitors to recover fragile constitutions from the brutalising effects of city smog, poor diet and even worse sanitation. From here, he sold aerated bottled Boscombe Spa water as a health tonic.

The area became increasingly popular and prosperous over the next few years, but local landowners and businessmen believed a pier was necessary if Boscombe was to really take off and rival Bournemouth. Calls for a pier were first aired in the local press in 1884 and by March the following year the Bournemouth Improvement Commissioners were prevailed upon to lay out plans. After a lengthy debate, the commissioners voted eight to five against developing a pier. They had just used large sums of public money to build Bournemouth Pier and were not prepared to build a second at Boscombe. They also saw that the chief beneficiaries of the new pier would be landowners like Sir Henry and Sir Percy Shelley.

At 8 p.m. on 17 March 1885 an extraordinary public meeting was held at the Hengistbourne Rooms in Drummond Road to consider the commissioners' refusal to sanction the pier. Local resident Henry Bazalgette proposed 'that the construction of a pier at Boscombe Chine is desirable to meet the requirements of

Boscombe Chine spring-water shelter became a popular meeting place in the 1870s. (Bournemouth Libraries)

the populous and rateable increase of this part of the Bournemouth Commissioners' District'. This was carried unanimously and the Boscombe Pier Co. was formed with a view to raising the necessary finances privately. Local lawyer and land agent to Sir Henry Drummond Wolff, Alexander McEwan Brown quickly assumed day to day direction of the company. Other members of the company committee included John Shepherd, manager of the Wilts & Dorset bank; Henry Bazalgette; Charles Rebbeck, honorary secretary of the Bournemouth Rowing Club; Dr James Hosker, a local surgeon who would later become Mayor of Bournemouth; and William Hoare, a prolific builder and also later mayor. By May, over £2,800 had been subscribed towards the pier but it was thought at least £8,000 would be needed.

The prospectus of the newly formed Boscombe Pier Co. was issued in July 1888, seeking capitalisation of £15,000 in the form of 3,000 shares valued at £5 each. Archibald Smith, who had designed Southbourne Pier, was tasked to design the new pier for Boscombe.

Sir Percy Shelley became the largest shareholder in the Boscombe Pier Co. Tenders for construction were issued soon after and the contract was finally awarded in September 1888 to Messrs Howell of Poole for a sum of £3,813. A further contract was awarded to Mr James Edwards of Southbourne for £938 to construct the Boscombe Pier Approach.

17 October 1888 was a big day for the residents of Boscombe as the start of pier construction was marked with a gala celebration. At around 10 a.m. in a field adjacent to Sea Road, a procession of children from St Clement's and Boscombe school led by mounted marshals together with detachments from the local fire brigade with their gleaming horse-drawn engine and a band of the Queen's Own Dorset Yeomanry Company, marched around the neighbourhood, down Christchurch Road and back towards the pier works. Lady Shelley and Sir Percy Shelley arrived at 12.30 p.m. and were received by the directors of the Boscombe Pier Co. to the cheer of local crowds. The first cast-iron screw pile weighing over 1 ton was ready, waiting to be driven into the beach with the aid of a wooden capstan. The capstan was attached by ropes to a small steam engine and Lady Shelley started the engine by pulling on a red silk ribbon. After a series of speeches the crowds cheered and maroons were fired off in celebration.

The sixty-six day labourers employed on the works were then treated to a meal and tobacco by visiting MP for Windsor, R. Richardson-Gardner. Meanwhile,

100 or so dignitaries attending the ceremony were invited to an altogether more elaborate meal in Boscombe Chine Gardens. Local school children were treated to the afternoon off school together with a bun and an orange.

During the golden age of pier building in the late nineteenth century, designing and building a pier was a relatively straightforward affair. All the cast-iron elements were prefabricated and could be ordered from a pattern book. However, casting techniques were not an exact science and the resulting variable quality often meant parts had to be sent back and cast again. No doubt construction on Boscombe Pier would have been hampered by attempts to drive the sometimes brittle cast-screw piles into ironstone rock which was found to be below the seabed. Rough seas also slowed work down. Nevertheless, the pier was completed within ten months at a final cost of £12,000.

A local newspaper recorded an incident in which two workmen engaged on the pier construction in July 1889 attempted to save a man from drowning. David Gowanlock, a painter and decorator and his friend George Absolom, a carpenter, went to Boscombe beach on Saturday 6 July to hire a rowing boat from Joseph Mildren who operated a concession on the beach. The two young men rowed out to a floating diving platform in the sea off the east side of the pier works. They undressed and went swimming. Soon after, George heard a cry and looked round in vain for his friend. Two workers on the pier saw David Gowanlock struggling in the water and cry out 'come and help me!' The workmen got hold of a grappling iron and rowed out to the spot in a boat to help, but they were too late. Gowanlock's body

Boscombe cast-iron pier as originally constructed, early 1890s. (Bournemouth Tourism)

Boscombe Beach looking west with Bournemouth Pier in the distance, 1890s. These bathing machines were owned and operated by the Boscombe Chine Hotel. The natural process of beach replenishment can be seen in the cliff slump behind. (Bournemouth Libraries)

washed up onto the beach fifteen minutes later. Dr Deans, a director of the Pier Co. and practicing physician, turned up later to declare the man dead. Aside from this, there had been no accidents or mishaps during the construction of the pier.

Initially the pier was intended to be only 400ft long, but this was extended during construction to 600ft, to allow for larger steam ships to pull in to the landing stages each side. The pier was 32ft wide and, like Southbourne Pier, featured two octagonal toll houses and turnstiles with a set of ornate gates at the entrance. The pier was declared fit for use by Lt Harston RN, the inspector appointed by the Board of Trade.

On Sunday 29 July the pier was officially opened by the Duke of Argyll and his son the Marquis of Lorne. They had travelled down from London by train with Gladstone, the Prime Minister, who was returning to his home at Hinton Admiral. Staying at the Chine Hotel, the Duke later recalled visiting Bournemouth forty years previously when it was little more than a village. Today, he marvelled at the crowds thronging the streets. An array of Chinese lanterns and Japanese umbrellas lined the route. 'The approach was thickly hung with flags on each side of the Sea Road for half its length,' reported the *Bournemouth Observer* newspaper. Various banners with

The mayor of Bournemouth, J.E. Beale, reopens Boscombe Pier in 1904, with the borough's first mayor, Mr T.J. Hankinson, staring out to camera. (*Bournemouth Graphic*)

mottos read: 'Advance Boscombe', 'Welcome to the Queen of the South' and 'Let Boscombe flourish'. Military bands and the Duke's own Pipers marched through the town and down to the pier in company with members of the Boscombe Club with their four-oared galley *Boscombe*. Crowds jostled around a small roped-off area for ticket holders only, in front of the pier. A second enclosure for the guests and dignitaries was laid out with a red carpet, a table and a high-backed armchair covered with a Scotch plaid shawl for the Duke. A guard of honour presented arms to the Duke and his son, hats were raised and cheers rang out.

In his address to the Duke, Mr Fisher, representing the Improvement Commissioners, glossed over their lack of support for the project, declaring:

> During the twelve or thirteen years that Boscombe has formed part of the Town of Bournemouth it has shared in the prosperity of the Town generally and had greatly increased in extent and population and the new Pier will doubtless greatly enhance its attractiveness and tend to a still greater increase in its development.

The Duke was presented with an album of photographic views of Boscombe and an address printed on vellum, which was initially objected to on the grounds of cost by Mr Trevanion of the Bournemouth Improvement Commissioners.

'I declare this pier open now, and let us take a short walk upon it,' announced the Duke. Over 10,000 people duly did so, generating takings of £40 on the first day. The steamship *Premier* ferried many of them back and forth to Bournemouth Pier throughout the day.

For lunch, the workmen were again treated to 'a satisfactory repast' of pork pies, bread, cheese, beer and tobacco in a tent off Sea Road, while the Duke and honoured guests dined in fine style at the Chine Hotel.

Various events were laid on throughout the rest of the day to entertain visitors and give a good glimpse of the kinds of seaside pleasures to be enjoyed at the time. Two galley races between rowing crews from Bournemouth and Boscombe took place while a duck hunt, no doubt using Joseph Mildren's rowing boats, occurred off the end of the pier. Bands played throughout the afternoon in the gardens. Meanwhile, 'Professor Ward, the talented swimming instructor of the Bournemouth baths, with his clever family, gave the exhibition of swimming and aquatic feats from the pier,' according to the local newspaper. At night, thousands of people wandered down Sea Road to admire the glowing Chinese lanterns lining the streets. They then watched a spectacular firework display at the beach.

Paddle steamers began regular connections to Bournemouth Pier and on 27 June 1897 the *Bonnie Princess* chartered from the Hastings and Eastbourne Steam Boat Co. carried passengers to watch the Naval Review of the Fleet of Spithead for Queen Victoria's Diamond Jubilee year.

The *Majestic* pleasure steamer off Bournemouth Pier, *c.* 1908. (*Bournemouth Tourism*)

Built by private enterprise, Boscombe Pier is regaled in Gala Dress on the occasion of reopening to the public under council ownership, 4 August 1904. (*Bournemouth Graphic*)

Boscombe Pier bandstand under construction in 1904. (John Cresswell)

Increasing numbers of visitors led to the construction of more hotels and guest houses, including the Boscombe Pier Hotel. A famous early resident of this hotel in the winter of 1896 was the young artist and friend of Oscar Wilde, Aubery Beardsley. He arrived in Boscombe suffering from the advanced stages of TB. Barely into his twenties, his most influential and scandalous work already behind him, his life had been reduced to 'bed and blood' according to a letter written to a friend. He considered himself 'an agonised wretch of depression, a poor shadow of the gay rococo thing' he had once been. Beardsley continued to work at night in his rooms, between two ormolu candlesticks, and read vociferously in bed during the day. In severe financial straits he wrote in August of being 'quite paralized by fear ... more or less in the mortal funk of a paupers life and death.' These feelings would no doubt have been shared by more than one of his fellow hotel guests. For many visitors to Bournemouth seafront, the sea and fresh air would have provided not so much a welcome respite as a final anguished glance towards the horizon.

It was while taking a walk down the Chine that Beardsley suffered a haemorrhage attack and collapsed. He barely made it back to his hotel. He died a few short years later aged twenty-five.

By 1902, the Boscombe Pier Co. was struggling financially. The high cost of building a pier could never be recouped and overtures were made to Bournemouth Council to take it over. The council had already taken on Boscombe Gardens three years previously for £8,000 so it was hoped a deal could be done. The council despatched its chief engineer Mr Lacey to assess the state of the pier. His report was not encouraging. 'The decking of the pier is rough and splintery,' there being 'no annual tarring and sanding of the same.' He went on to state, 'the pier generally requires overhauling and thoroughly scraping and painting in every part' and would require over £4,000 being spent on it. When the Pier Co. proposed terms, they were initially refused before a sale agreement was reached for the sum of £9,000 in September 1903.

On the morning of Saturday 26 September, Charles Basket, the pier master, unlocked the turnstiles and waited for F.P. Dolamore, the council's assistant engineer, to arrive and inspect matters before formally taking over. The *Majestic*, the last steamer of the season, was due to dock four days later and the council had made no commitment to retaining the existing staff beyond that. So it would be with some apprehension that the pier porters J. Shergold, M. Rogers and J. Perkins together with brothers Thomas and Herbert French, employed as boatmen, lined up to meet Mr Dolamore.

Dolamore meticulously noted the fixtures and fittings on the pier, including a damaged nine-rung ladder, sixteen signal flags in bad repair and twelve musical stands. There was also an 'automatic machine' licensed on payment of 15 per cent profits.

As soon as the season ended the small octagonal bandstand on the end of the pier was removed and in 1906 it was re-erected in the children's corner at King's Park where it still stands today.

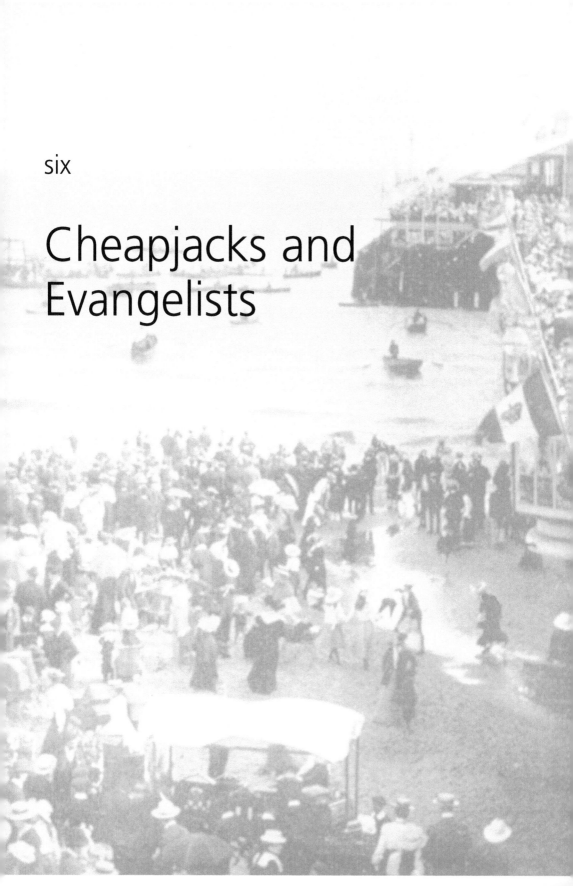

six

Cheapjacks and
Evangelists

For most of the nineteenth century local commentators had been lamenting the poor standard of public morals and behaviour on the beach. The first generation of wealthier visitors could be relied upon to dress with dignity at all times, parading on the pier or sauntering along the beach dressed to the nines carrying elegant parasols. Sea bathing was conducted in private and mostly away from view or from bathing machines. In the quieter nooks and chines, nude bathing was not uncommon, particularly amongst men, but there were few people around to complain in any case.

Things started to change when the South-Western railway line arrived in 1870. The journey time from London came down to three-and-a-half hours and this proved a massive stimulus for the development of the town. Hand in hand with an exponential growth in population over the next few decades came a new type of eager visitor looking for pleasure and a chance to let off steam from the drudgery of everyday life.

The lower middle and working classes who came in their thousands brought a spirit of subversive carnival to the seaside. Most sought the idle pleasures of walking or picnicking on the beach. Some came to try their hand at swimming. Modern swimming for recreation and heath was beginning to catch on with books devoted to the subject and public demonstrations by accomplished swimmers.

The bathing machines were too expensive to hire and too slow and cumbersome for most people and there were never enough machines to satisfy demand anyway. Many bathers simply began to bring changing tents or continued to bathe in the nude, to the annoyance of many.

The sleepy beach started to become a crowded and noisy place at times, especially around the piers.

Against this backdrop, *Butcher & Cole's Directory* of 1874 countered that the resort should remain the preserve of a better class of visitor, noting 'Bournemouth is a name which is now familiar to everyone moving in the best circles of society, as that of a resort not only ranked with the most fashionable watering-places, but justly valued on account of its delightful quiet and retirement.' This was a vision of a sleepy and refined resort. A vision echoed by many of the town's elders who attempted to impose a sense of dignity to the beach, avoiding the gaudy reputations of other seaside towns. At first there seemed little to be done for other than the piers, the beach was largely unregulated.

On 28 June 1883 the Improvement Commissioners passed the first bathing rights in an effort to control proceedings:

Alum Chine, Bournemouth.

Above: Alum Chine Beach in the 1920s Unknown postcard. (Bournemouth Libraries)

Left: Bathing machines ranged along the sands, c 1890s Stalls on the beach sold fresh fruit and lemonade. The impromptu auditorium of chairs arranged in a horseshoe would have been used by beach entertainers. (Leisure Services)

It is recommended in all cases of bathing [that] suitable bathing drawers be insisted upon. That persons be allowed to bathe from the landing stage of the Pier between the hours of 6 a.m. and 8 a.m. That no bathing whatever be allowed from the shore between the Steps Chine to the East of the Pier and Joseph's Steps to the West of the Pier, except from bathing machines. That beyond the shore limits to the east and west boundary of the District persons be permitted to bathe from the shore up to 9 a.m. and after 7 p.m. That bathing be allowed within the last mentioned limits up to 11 a.m. and after 6 p.m. from tents or from inclosing screens. Such screens to be not less than 6 ft high. That a man be employed for the management of bathing up to 11 a.m.

In part these recommendations, which were largely unenforceable for the beach was still private property at this time, were possibly drawn up under pressure from the bathing-machine operators eager to reassert their control over public bathing. It may be sheer coincidence that one of the hoteliers and bathing-machine owners and an Improvement Commissioner shared the name Joseph Cutler!

The old guard tried to impose their ideas for a refined and genteel beach by establishing the Bournemouth Club on a prime site next to Bournemouth Pier, where the Oceanarium stands today. This imposing stone building was the model of a Victorian Gentleman's club. Built in 1871 this men-only institution featured a quiet dimly lit lounge, bar and billiard rooms. Even at is peak there were never more than 300 members and, in 1874, admission for visitors could only be secured through nomination by an existing member of the club to the club committee which met once a week.

Amazingly, the club survived right through the golden age of the resort, until by 1959 there were barely 100 members, periodically sipping drinks and reading the papers with the noise and bustle of tens of thousands of holidaymakers right outside their windows. The club house was finally raised to the ground in 1966, but the space remained empty for a further thirty years and is still referred to as Red Square after the colour of the exposed painted cliff-retaining walls left behind.

Clubs were a defining aspect of the Victorian era and every conceivable form of leisure activity on the beach spawned a club of some sort. Amateur swimming and rowing clubs were some of the earliest on the seafront. The YMCA offered a range of sporting activities based around a boathouse on the sand, located to the west of Bournemouth Pier where the present-day Happylands amusements building stands. By 1900 they had over ten boats and organised regular water-polo games and swimming competitions.

Sands from Pier West, Bournemouth

Bournemouth West Beach, showing the Bournemouth Club House on the promenade to the right. This is now the site of the Oceanarium. Unknown postcard, early 1900s. (Bournemouth Library)

At Boscombe, a new rowing club was started in 1912. The Reverend E.J. Kennedy presided over it with a membership of fifty regulars. Annual subscriptions cost 10s and their first boat was bought with a £10 donation from Mr Hayes and named 'The Direct'. Their sailing colours were blue and white.

The Westover rowing club which still operates from their original premises to the west of Bournemouth Pier also dates back to the nineteenth century.

Fishing clubs became popular too. The Boscombe and Southbourne Sea Fishing Club, founded in 1918, operated off Boscombe Pier. Their first president was Gordon Selfridge, owner of the celebrated London store, who lived in a grand house the edge of Hengistbury Head. The club's first competition took place on the end of Boscombe Pier on 23 October 1918 and from then on they regularly competed with a club based at Bournemouth Pier.

Southbourne Pier was noted as the best location for catching plaice and occasionally turbot and bass in the 1890s. Bait and hooks could be purchased from boatmen on the beach. Meanwhile, Durley and Middle Chine beaches were considered good for whiting, and boats could be hired there to fish further out in the bay. Fresh fish was often sold near the entrance to the piers. Bournemouth's last small-scale commercial fisherman still operates from Durley Chine Beach and, if you are lucky to spot him, fresh fish can be purchased from the beach early in the day.

Gypsy fairs and entertainments on the beach east of Bournemouth Pier became an increasingly familiar sight on bank holidays from the 1880s on, as chancers and entrepreneurs eagerly sought to capitalise on the holiday crowds. A typical Victorian beach fair would feature coconut shies, helter-skelters, swings and roundabouts. All around would be 'hawkers, cheapjacks and evangelists raucously trying to attract attention,' according to one newspaper report. By 1890 octagonal wooden kiosks were sited on the beach selling everything from bananas and lemonade to puppy dogs. Disabled sailors sold buckets and spades from another stall. Pony stands were positioned either side of the pier and so too were temporary stages advertising concert parties such as 'Birchmore and Linden's Pierrots' and 'the Gay Cadets'.

The Bournemouth Regatta Committee line up outside the Rowing Club on the West Beach, August 1904. (*Bournemouth Graphic*)

Bournemouth Regatta, 18 August 1904. Throughout most of the twentieth century this was the principal seaside event of the season. The regatta in 1904 featured rowing, sailing and swimming races, a lifeboat demonstration, a water-polo match and shoreline sports. Children took part in a decorated boat competition. (*Bournemouth Graphic*)

Meanwhile, dozens of rowing boats large and small were available for hire either side of Bournemouth and Boscombe Piers.

Bournemouth finally gained borough status in 1890 and further self-governing powers in 1900. The new council was now in a position to exert direct influence over the free for all on the beach. Strict controls were introduced on beach trading and public behaviour. Women were told to wear 'suitable costume or dress, consisting of a tunic or blouse reaching from neck to knees, with belt and knickerbocker drawers.'

The council also began negotiations with the various private landowners who owned the beach. A large portion of the cliffs and foreshore around Bournemouth was finally leased to the council from the Meryick Estate on a 999-year lease commencing Christmas day 1902 on condition that no buildings would be erected or altered without the consent of the Meyrick Estate – a condition that still applies today.

August bank holiday amusement fair on the beach, east of Bournemouth Pier, *c.* 1890. The travelling fair was an important part of the entertainment offered to late Victorian visitors to Bournemouth. Once the promenade was built in 1907 it became no longer feasible to stage the fair, although echoes of this can still be found on the amusement rides at Pier Approach today. (Bournemouth Libraries)

Bournemouth celebrates its Incorporation Day in 1890 against the iconic backdrop of Bournemouth Pier entrance. (Bournemouth Libraries)

seven

The Tale of the Boscombe Whale

Whilst negotiating direct control of the seafront, council members would have recalled a strange incident which took place at the beginning of 1897 which highlighted some of the problems they faced.

On Tuesday 5 January 1897 a tramp steamer was passing the coast off Southbourne when it rode over and broke the back of a whale that had come in close to the shore. That night the dead whale was spotted washed ashore near Fisherman's Walk and over the next two days the ebbing tide carried it down as far as Boscombe Pier. The magnificent animal was 70ft long and quickly drew an excited crowd of people who had never seen anything like it before. The coastguard was the first on scene and they rather grandly annexed the creature in the name of the Crown. To this day, any whale washed ashore is deemed the property of the monarch.

The coastguard tried and failed to effectively secure the animal and a debate began as to how to dispose of the whale which was estimated to weigh 40 tonnes. Some suggested towing it out to sea while others wanted to auction it off. Meanwhile, local schoolmasters gave open-air lectures to children and their interested parents. In the evening some boys came back and took running jumps up its black slippery sides and tobogganed back down again. Three days later, over 500 people gathered around the whale, with heavy rain teeming down. The coastguard conducted an auction on behalf of Her Majesty's Receiver of Wrecks. Speculation was running high as to how much it would sell for and who would buy it. In the event, the sheer size of the animal and the difficulty and expense that would be necessary to remove it put many potential bidders off. The first offer was £5 and eventually the whale was knocked down for £27 to Dr Spencer Simpson, a Bournemouth GP.

He wrote out a cheque addressed to the Queen and announced his intentions to boil the whale's skeleton and turn a profit from displaying it and giving lectures.

By the next day, word had travelled far and train loads of curious visitors started arriving in Boscombe to view the whale. The police had to be called down to keep the crowds back. Meanwhile, Dr Simpson was busy recruiting workmen skilled in the art of cutting up whales. Rather predictably, he was struggling to find anyone up to the job.

As the weekend rolled into the following week, the council began to get nervous. The carcass was beginning to decay. Work started haphazardly to cut the flesh from the bones. The men didn't have the tools or the stomach for the job. The stench forced them to wear bandanas over their faces and disinfectant had to be sprayed continuously, while the public continued to gawp and get in the way. Council officials demanded to know how much longer Dr Simpson was going to take to get rid of the whale.

By now, the whale had sunk deep into the sand and was surrounded by large pools of water where attempts had been made to excavate it. There was a spirit of excitement in the air tinged with incomprehension and awe as more and more people turned up to watch. Over 300 tickets were sold on one afternoon train from Christchurch to Boscombe alone. Some came from even farther afield. One farm labourer travelled all the way from Somerset to see this 'wonder of the deep'. He walked all around the whale before climbing up on top. 'What are you going to do?' asked a bystander. 'Do? I've come vorty mile to see this 'ere whale, and I'm going to walk on 'im from 'is 'ead to 'is tail.' The man began to walk atop the whale but quickly sank through the decaying flesh and had to be extracted from his predicament by onlookers.

Simpson was forced to pay for police cover to keep people back, but he could only afford to hire one officer. Work continued slowly and two days later a snow storm blew up and the lighters had to return to port. Simpson's forty-eight hour period of grace was over.

Over the weekend, Mr Cooper the chief sanitary inspector from the council turned up and ordered his men to shovel sand over the rotting flesh and bones which greatly dismayed Simpson's taxidermist who arrived from Brighton. Mr Cooper then returned to the scene intending to carry away the whale with the aid of some corporation carts. Simpson, with the full backing of the coastguard, defied the council to touch his property at their peril. Cooper and his carts left empty-handed.

Over the next few days the bones were successfully removed and transported by luggage train to Brighton to be cleaned and cured ready for display. The ineffectual council officials were made fun of when a sign appeared next to the rotting blubber on the beach, reading: 'Whale, 3d per lb; all sold; Corporation too.'

Cooper returned five days later on 18 January with a large retinue of assistants and horse-drawn carts, determined to forcibly remove the whale from the beach. Simpson arrived shortly afterwards, vigorously protesting as the council officials removed 25 tons of flesh. At some point Simpson drew a sword-stick at Mr Cooper and threatened to run him through. A policeman had to forcibly remove the weapon from him.

The coastguard officer, meanwhile, stood on a remaining piece of flesh, refusing to be moved. Cooper demanded the man to step off the whale but the coastguard fellow simply stood there smoking his clay pipe in defiance. Cooper

Police keep enthusiastic crowds back as they inspect the whale on the beach at Boscombe in January 1897. (Bournemouth Libraries)

turned to a handful of burly labourers with spades and forks for assistance and the coastguard man quickly backed down under protest.

On 25 January, Dr Simpson was charged in court with assault on Mr Cooper. Simpson was facing a gaol sentence of two months. In the event he was fined £1 plus costs.

Most of the blubber was eventually dumped off Brownsea Island, but a quantity found its way to Poole Quay to be auctioned at the King's Arms on 30 January. Despite the sale being widely advertised, Mr Curtis the auctioneer, Simpson and a newspaper reporter found themselves alone. Three-quarters of an hour later a handful of seafarers had turned up out of curiosity and the auction began. Curtis worked hard to drum up bids, extolling the importance of blubber for manure and soap. Simpson had spent £135 to get the blubber to Poole Quay but it finally sold for a paltry 5s.

The whale skeleton was eventually mounted on a frame and displayed on Boscombe Pier. It weathered a few seasons before being removed in 1904 and was last seen piled in a heap in the backyard of Powell's marine store in Victoria Road, Springbourne.

The local authorities came to fisticuffs with the owner of the whale over removing the animal from the beach in January 1897. (Bournemouth Libraries)

The whale's skeleton was finally displayed as an attraction on Boscombe pier until 1904. Children took great delight in climbing its bleached bones and sliding down them. (Bournemouth Libraries)

eight

The Golden Age
of the Pier

Britain's seaside piers and the pleasure steamers that operated from them enjoyed their heyday in the years leading up to the First World War and Bournemouth Pier was no exception.

Mr Benjamin Pond writing in 1962 recalled visiting the pier as a boy during this time:

> For a pier toll of two pence I could spend all day on Bournemouth Pier and see three variety shows and hear three Municipal orchestras. Before the First World War there were eight regular steamers running from the pier and you could sail round the Isle of Wight for only three shillings. To avoid paying even 2d some of us would climb the ironwork on the beach and creep through the network of cross-girders, thus reaching the seaward underdeck. I remember one very cold winter when an elderly man clad only in a bathing costume would ride a bicycle from off a plank and plunge into the icy sea. He did this daily, and each time he climbed back on to the pier he would stand and talk for thirty minutes or more on life-saving. Meanwhile the audience, in heavy winter attire, stood shivering like jellyfish. An air bladder was fixed to the bicycle to prevent it sinking, and one of the pier staff would fish the machine out of the water after each dive.

The pier had proved immensely successful since it opened in 1880. The *Argosy* periodical in 1881 described it as:

> Wide, new and well-built, a place where one might pace up and down and enjoy the beauties of sunrise and sunset, with the restless sea moving and surging around. In the autumn, few would use it as the visitors are most of them too delicate to venture thereon except when the midday sun has dispersed all chilliness from the atmosphere.

In its first year of operation, the pier generated revenue of £2,225 and by 1887 over half a million visitors paid to enter the pier, generating around £3,528. One of the many visitor guides outlined the:

> Abundance of opportunity for agreeable excursions . . . afforded by the Bournemouth Steampacket Company's steamboat and numerous other well-appointed steamboats, which ply almost daily during the summer months from Bournemouth Pier to some distant spot along the coast, voyaging at times a far west as Lulworth, Weymouth and Portland, and east to Ryde, Cowes, Ventnor, Alum Bay, etc., Portsmouth and the neighbourhood. Due notice is given of

Bournemouth Pier Approach in 1908 with the pier entrance building in the background. This was a popular carriage drop-off point. (Bournemouth Tourism)

these excursions at the Pier Toll office, by advertisements in the local press, bills issued and exhibited in the town, which contain every particular, and by the public Crier.

In 1893 the pier was extended in length by a further 300ft under the design and guidance of Frank E. Robinson. The pier was now 1,000ft long and could accommodate more steam vessels than before.

By 1901 the numbers of steamers operating had increased massively. The *Bournemouth Guardian* newspaper estimated that on August bank holiday that year, 'it has been computed that on the ten steamers plying during the day from Bournemouth Pier, there can hardly have been less than 10,000 persons embarked.' Tickets to sail to watch King Edward VII's Coronation Naval Review at Spithead in June 1902 were so popular that the *Majestic* and *Monarch* steamers sold out a week before sailing. Cosens, the boats' operators, announced in the press that they were bringing a third steamer, the *Victoria*, to take extra passengers.

So many steamers were operating and competing against each other that certain boats would unofficially race each other home. In 1902 the *Cambria* and *Balmoral* found themselves returning to Bournemouth from an excursion to Cherbourg. Word got round that both vessels were expected at the same time. A big crowd gathered on the end of Bournemouth Pier and wagered money on which vessel would get back first. The *Cambria*, by far the fastest steamer in the bay, won.

By 1908 over 50,000 people embarked on steamer excursions in August alone. And over 90,000 people disembarked at the pier. So heavy was demand that the landing stages had to be widened that winter to accommodate all the passengers waiting to board.

The business of the pier was presided over by a pier master who would frequently be an ex-naval officer, like Captain Newman who held the post in 1903. Dressed in full uniform and peak cap he was a figure of authority with a detailed knowledge of seamanship – a very necessary skill with so many vessels birthing, sometimes two abreast. The last of the old pier masters survived well into the 1960s.

Facilities on the pier were expanded upon to include a pagoda bandstand, and bench seating was erected on the end of the pier, together with a newspaper stall and refreshment kiosk. The Municipal Orchestra and various military bands played most days to large crowds. Electric lighting was also added to illuminate the pier at night. The pier had evolved from a simple landing stage and promenading deck into a centre for seaside entertainment.

Hard-wearing teak decking was installed on the pier head to facilitate the craze for roller-skating during the winter months. A spring board was provided on the end of the pier for diving off and regular exhibitions of diving and swimming were provided by the likes of Mr S.L. Smith. The practice of Bournemouth to Boscombe Pier swims was also established and these still go strong today.

An early exhibition of flying took place between the piers in July 1912. The *Daily Mail*-sponsored hydroplane thrilled the crowds over two days with the pilot offering to take anyone up with him. For this exhibition, the council agreed a payment of 50 per cent of the day's pier takings, not to exceed £100.

The thriving business at Bournemouth was in some contrast to the struggling fortunes of Boscombe Pier.

The Bournemouth Corporation took ownership of Boscombe Pier at the end of the 1903 season for a sum of £9,000. Over the winter a further £3,380 was spent on repairs and refurbishments. The pier was completely repainted and a new larger bandstand erected. The entrance area was roofed over with public lavatories installed. With a disappointing £42 in tolls collected for 1903, a packed programme of events was planned by the council to attract the crowds the following year.

A section of the Municipal band under conductor Mr Hollis was engaged to play on the pier twice a day from June to September. Band members were each issued with a black mackintosh cloak to protect them in wet weather.

Enjoying the Breezes, cartoon dated September 1904 by Fell.
Bournemouth Pier is satirised here as the haunt of sickly youths
and colonial types recuperating from a spell in the tropics.
(*Bournemouth Graphic*)

Visitors arriving at the beach might stop for an ice cream from E. Hutchins'
stall or purchase refreshments from Emma Stripp. John Harris was on hand to take
their souvenir photograph while H.H. Nicholls entertained them with his Black &
Whites concert party on the beach to the west of the pier. Bath chairs and cycles
could be hired and on a sunny day visitors might catch H. Counter and his pupils
giving a gymnastic display of Swedish club exercises and vaulting horse on the pier.
And if that did not tickle their fancy there was always Podmore Clark and pupils

playing popular tunes on the banjo. To begin with, business was brisk and by the end of the year William Newman, the pier master, had collected £133 8s 1d in tolls.

To cater for the growing crowds, a refreshment shelter was built on the beach to the west of the pier in 1906 and operated by Messrs Goldsworthy and Voysey. And public shelters were added in 1915, offering a 'sheltered and cool resting place in sight of the pier and sea.'

But despite council investment the pier was still not producing a profit and by 1910 required a further £4,000 worth of repairs to the pier head where 'several piles have gone down and the main structure is much out of level.' And four years later the landing stages were in a poor state.

Boats continued to ply from the pier. By 1913 the *Monarch*, *Balmoral* and *Brighton Queen* were offering regular sailings. Passengers totalled 52,800 either travelling to or from the pier that August – but that was less than half the number of passengers embarking from Bournemouth Pier.

The weather had been poor on August bank holiday Monday 1912. Storms two nights previously had whipped up and destroyed many of the beach tents leaving

Celebrating Queen Victoria's Diamond Jubilee on Bournemouth Pier, 1897. (Bournemouth Libraries)

The Home Fleet off Bournemouth, early 1900s. (Bournemouth Libraries)

wreckage everywhere. On the bank holiday barely 2,659 people paid to enter the pier which generated a meagre income of £22 12s 11d. By contrast, over 22,816 people had walked onto Bournemouth Pier that same day. In a desperate effort to recoup some of their losses, Sunday concerts were permitted to take place on Boscombe Pier. Entertainments on a Sunday had, up to this point, been vigorously refused by the towns' moral guardians. The anticipated chaos and depravity failed to materialise and Sunday concerts on both piers became an established feature from then on.

Concert parties on the beach close by attempted to rouse some cheer among a loyal following of visitors eager to escape the throning crowds at Bournemouth. 'The entertainments given by Les Vivandieres are very good and most enjoyable,' reported the *Bournemouth Graphic* in June 1912. The band was conducted by Mr Douglas Gordon and saw 'a better class of patron than formerly.' Meanwhile, Mr Reuben More's concert party attracted a crowd on Monday evening. 'The party consisted of song, chorus, duet and humorous element.' The finale featured a song called 'Brighton by the Sea' by the whole party. Those taking part were Messrs R. Currie, R. More, A. Godfrey, Tinker and Misses F. Driver and Eva Godfrey.

Bournemouth Pier illuminated at night in 1904. Light shows and firework displays off the pier have always attracted the crowds. (*Bournemouth Graphic*)

The *Daily Mail* hydroplane entertains the crowds over Bournemouth Seafront in June 1912. The pilot offered to 'take up' anyone who was interested. He was paid half the days takings from Bournemouth & Boscombe Piers. (*Bournemouth Graphic*)

Mr Hickman-Smith's Royal Entertainers performing on Boscombe Pier, summer 1912. Hickman-Smith is the one at the top. (*Bournemouth Graphic*)

With an increasingly unsustainable share of the holiday trade, matters were about to change radically with proposals to complete a promenade linking Bournemouth with Boscombe. The scheme was vigorously opposed by the steamboat operators and it is not hard to understand why. When it was completed the viability of steamer services from Boscombe Pier was undermined overnight and plans to extend the length of the landing stages at Boscombe to increase capacity were immediately shelved.

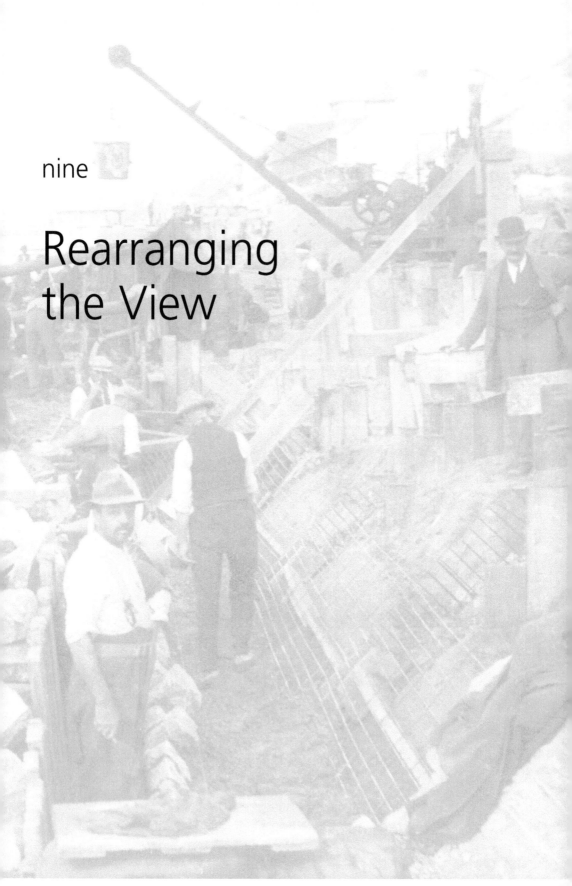

nine

Rearranging the View

The coastline around Bournemouth has been in fast retreat for thousands of years. A glance at the different coloured horizontal layers of gravel, sand and clay in the cliffs reveals the reason why. Rainwater and spring water percolates freely through the gravel and sand layers then becomes trapped when it reaches the clay. The build up of water on this layer acts as a lubricant, causing the softer layers above to landslide. In this way the beach was constantly replenished with sand from the cliffs every time there was a landslip. Without the replenishment of sand the beach would have simply washed away through the action of the waves and wind. The phenomenon of longshore drift sees the wind and waves predominantly coming in from the south-west, dragging the beach eastwards towards Hengistbury Head.

For thousands of years Hengistbury Head acted as a bulwark with its impermeable ironstone coastline, regulating the loss of beach further west towards Bournemouth. But when the ironstone was quarried away in the mid-nineteenth century, the head itself started to erode at a fast rate and aided the longshore drift of sand from Bournemouth straight past Hengistbury.

Of course, by the end of the nineteenth century the cliff tops along Bournemouth had been largely built upon as the town expanded. It has been calculated that up to 3ft of land was lost on the cliff top each year, inching ever closer to property and roads. Sudden landslips occurred frequently and cliff-top footpaths had to constantly be remade.

By the beginning of the twentieth century the Borough Engineers Dept, who had been given responsibility for the cliffs and foreshore as well as the piers, tried various experiments to halt the massive erosion. Early attempts involved digging large holes in the cliff top and filling them with broken stone and clinker to channel rain and spring water down to drainage pipes coming horizontally out of the cliffs. Later, the exposed cliffs were extensively planted in an effort to slow the process of wind-blown erosion. Various types of vegetation including many semi-tropical plants were tried but only a few took root. One of the most successful was Hottentot fig, which today is considered an invasive weed and now constant attempts are made to cut it back.

Today the cliffs are covered in large areas with a wide variety of vegetation, some of which was planted and others self-seeded. Rare flora and fauna abound to the extent that much of the cliffs have been designated Sites of Special Scientific Interest – an unexpected, but positive consequence of the town's attempt to halt erosion over 100 years ago.

Later experiments towards the mid-twentieth century involved extensive regrading of the cliff slope back to a 45-degree angle in an effort to halt the threat of land slippage. A careful glance along the cliffs will quickly reveal where the slope has been regraded and where areas of untouched craggy outcrop remain.

Turning their attention to the base of the cliff which was most vulnerable to the action of the waves, the engineers resolved to build a defensive sea wall, with the addition of a promenade to ease access and enhance the attraction of the beach for visitors. Chief among supporters for this scheme was the Bournemouth Hotels Interest Association who saw a sheltered Undercliff Drive as a great benefit for the invalid visitors who made Bournemouth their home during the winter months. Plans were drawn up and the first section running from Bournemouth Pier to Meyrick Steps, now called East Cliff Zig-Zag, was built costing £16,000 and opened in 1907.

Dan Godfrey, the celebrated Director of Music for the Municipal Orchestra and later founder of the Bournemouth Symphony Orchestra, recalled the German Emperor Kaiser Wilhelm staying at nearby Highcliff Castle in 1907. He decided one day to go for a spin in his motor car along the Undercliff Drive from Bournemouth heading towards Boscombe. He is supposed to have turned purple with rage upon discovering that the 'road' only took him as far as the East Cliff lift. History does not record whether the Kaiser eventually made it to Boscombe.

The promenade and sea wall was then extended to Boscombe Pier in 1911 at a further cost of £45,000, providing a through road. The Bournemouth end was not pedestrianised and shut off to traffic until 1973.

F.P. Dolamore, the borough engineer, writing in 1919 recalled the construction of the Undercliff Drive extending 1½ miles between the two piers:

There is a carriage drive 30 feet wide and a promenade 20 feet wide on the seaward side at an elevation of 7 feet above high water or about 10 feet above mean tide level. Steps are provided at intervals along the length of the promenade which follow the slope of the inclined wall, giving easy access to the beach. There are several circular projecting bays along the length of the wall which break up the outline of the drive and promenade. In addition to the steps there are sloping ways giving access to the beach for bathing machines, boats, etc. Both the drive and promenade are formed on sand and gravel filling obtained from the beach and cliffs. It will be seen that by the form of construction adopted, any waves striking the (sea) wall will run gently up the slope, and the force is thereby spent. The slope of the wall is 1 in 2.

Boscombe East promenade and sea wall under construction, 12 August 1926. (Leisure Services)

Bournemouth Pier Approach looking down from the East Cliff slope, c.1880s. Perhaps the seated gentleman is inspecting his paper for the times of the next pleasure-steamer sailings. (Bournemouth Libraries)

But having built a strong wall to resist erosion caused by the tides, Dolamore encountered a new problem, 'As it was found that the sand was considerably eroded in front of the Drive it was decided to erect groynes. These have been constructed on a novel plan in reinforced concrete.' These concrete groynes were made with sections of railway line at the core and were designed to halt the beach drifting away. An extensive system of groynes is still in use today.

With the Undercliff Drive built, the council seized the opportunity to create further amenities for visitors to enjoy and recoup some income towards the massive sums borrowed to build the seawall and promenade. Dolamore explained in an address to the Institution of Municipal Engineers in 1919:

The author has taken great interest in the working of the foreshore enterprise, and has been responsible from its inception, which has been entirely built up in the last ten years. 160 bungalows have been constructed by our own staff and let at £12 10 per annum and there is a waiting list of over a hundred would-be tenants. Construction had however to be entirely abandoned during the war. Deck chairs are let at various points at a charge of one penny. Three refreshment rooms and several stall pitches are let out by tender. Free public bathing is allowed at certain hours and patrols are provided for the public safety. Public bathing is also provided at a charge during the day at several fixed points and a large business is done. We took over from a previous lessee a good number of the old type of wheeled bathing machines, but as they fall out of commission we are constructing improved appliances. We have constructed some hundreds of tents on wooden frames which can be taken to pieces and which are mounted on small sledges. This has proved most successful and is easily handled. For the idea we are indebted to the Margate Authorities. I have designed cubicles for use on the sea wall slope, of a type which can be entirely taken to pieces and stored when not in use in the bathing offices and drying sheds. A model is on view and they can be seen in place when you visit the drive. The public are also allowed to erect tents at a small rental, subject to the tents being of a standard type and size.

The bungalows, or beach huts, were of the same design and specification to those in use today. Most of the current huts were built in the 1950s and 1960s; a smaller proportion date to the 1930s and one or two may be originals from 1909. This is the earliest reference to purpose-built municipal beach huts in the UK and it is known that a number of resorts based their huts on the Bournemouth models designed by Mr Dolamore.

Cartoon showing construction of the Undercliff Drive and sea wall in 1907 with Mr Lacey, the borough engineer as King Canute, resisting the tide. (*Bournemouth Graphic*)

The very term bungalow conjured up an image of sophisticated leisure with a hint of the subtropical to Edwardian visitors. Today the name does not have quite the same ring. Indeed, visitors in recent years have been greatly confused as to what a beach bungalow might actually be and were slightly disappointed to find a wooden hut with four deckchairs and no overnight sleeping permitted!

Notice also the reference to all the huts and deckchairs being built by the council's own direct labour force. Until as late as the 1980s the council still employed gangs of men to make deckchairs and the present Seafront Ranger Team spend part of the closed winter season repairing damaged deckchair stock to this day.

Undercliff Drive in 1907 showing the Meyrick Steps, now known as East Cliff Zig-Zag. Unknown postcard. (Bournemouth Libraries)

Back in 1919 these new amenities proved hugely popular, generating significant income for the council. Deckchairs took £2,900, tent sites £1,100, bathing machines £3,500 and refreshment stalls £1,600. Nearly ninety years later the proportions of beach spend on deckchairs compared to spend on food and drink have inversed to quite a considerable degree.

The final major pieces of infrastructure to be built before the First World War were the East and West Cliff Lifts, either side of Bournemouth Pier. Concession was secured from the Meyrick Estate in July 1905 to construct a, 'hydraulic lift, enabling the Public commodiously to ascend from the level of the beach to the top of the East Cliff by licence.' The Meyrick estate was paid an annual rental of £25 by the council.

The East Cliff Lift built by Messrs Waygood Ltd was opened by Lady Meyrick on 16 April 1908. The two lift cars were originally designed to carry up to ten passengers each and ran on rails, technically classifying them as a railway. An electrically powered winding drum raised and lowered the cars then as now. The lift travels a distance of 35m up the cliff at a speed, these days, of ½m per second.

The Undercliff Drive as built in 1907, looking east from Bournemouth Pier. (Leisure Services)

The sands looking east of Bournemouth Pier, c. 1908. The Bournemouth East toilets were under construction and a space had been cleared beyond it, waiting for the first beach bungalows to be built. The boats in the foreground were available for pleasure hire. (Bournemouth Tourism)

Constructing the East Cliff Lift in 1908. (Leisure Services)

Right: East Cliff Lift prior to opening in 1908. The lift cabins were made to the same design as tram cars. New cars were fitted in 2008, marking its 100th anniversary. (Leisure Services)

Below: A packed beach looking east from a steamer coming into Bournemouth Pier in 1922. From left to right: the large white structure on the beach next to the pier is the back of the sand sculpture display hut; the sculpture could be viewed from the pier. The Belle Vue Hotel sits on the site of the future Pavilion with Sydenham's Marine Library & Baths adjacent. The Undercliff cloisters, still a feature in existence today, with the East Beach Cafe. The East Cliff toilets sit next to that, with the line of beach bungalows beyond. The beach itself is lined with collapsible changing boxes. (Bournemouth Tourism)

Work on the West Cliff Lift commenced slightly later and opened on 1 August 1908. Not only is this lift slightly bigger, with the cars carrying up to sixteen passengers, but it runs ever so slightly faster at 1.43m per second! Numerous upgrades of the lift cars have taken place over the years, often using converted coach bodies. Most recently the East Cliff Lift has had new stainless-steel cars fitted in the winter of 2007, designed by the Bournemouth Arts Institute. A further cliff lift was later built at Fisherman's Walk in 1935.

Over the course of little more than thirty years the council had spent vast sums of money transforming the natural splendour of the coast into something even better, designed to cater for the holidaymaker's every need. The guidebooks marvelled at the value that had been added to the coast and in the process the landscape of the seafront had changed utterly.

By the start of the First World War all of the principal elements of beach infrastructure were in place. 1914 was a great summer. The beaches were crowded and business had never been better. The coming war would cast a long shadow on people's attitudes to life that extended even to the way they took their holidays. Holidaymakers after the war changed and the beach would have to adapt and change with them.

ten

Here Comes
the Sun

Bournemouth, with its reputation for convalescence in the winter sun, became a hospital by the sea for the physically and mentally traumatised troops chewed up by the endless conflict in France. The piers and promenades filled with men in uniform and attendant nurses. The entertainments and attractions remained open throughout the conflict. And perhaps for a brief few days, service men on leave could forget the horrors that awaited them back at the front and enjoy some of the pre-war certainties of a good day out at the seaside.

A determination to enjoy the moment marked out the post-war mood. The stuffiness of dress and formality of manners were rejected and people started to look for more sophisticated forms of holiday entertainment. The beach was still a huge draw with more and more visitors coming to Bournemouth. A walk on the pier was pleasant. A trip on a boat round the bay was enjoyable. But what they really wanted now was music to dance to and sun to worship. Most of all, they wanted the sun.

The cult of sunbathing, still very much at the heart of our own culture today, goes back to Adolf Just in late nineteenth-century Germany as a medicinal cure known as heliotherapy for a broad range of illnesses and in particular TB. The idea was taken up in the UK after the war and promised the same health benefits that doctors had been claiming for sea bathing half a century earlier. Lazing in the sun and acquiring a radiant tan also became extraordinarily fashionable, inspired by Hollywood movies.

The healthy, outdoor life was celebrated and encouraged with a never ending programme of sports and gymnastics demonstrations on the beach. The old baths and Sydenham's book shop were finally replaced with a modern public swimming pool. The Pier Approach Baths opened in March 1937 and cost £80,000 to build. Inside was a 100ft by 35ft swimming pool. Aquatic displays, swimming trials and galas were held every week and doors along one entire side of the baths could be opened out to let in the sea breezes. A solarium and sun-bathing terrace were also constructed.

The old Victorian bathing machines had become redundant. People would get changed in their cars before dashing off into the water, much to the annoyance of council officials. The last bathing machines were broken up by 1930 and replaced with new hygienic bathing stations. The Happylands Arcade to the west of Bournemouth Pier is a rare survivor of a 1930s bathing station. With shelters for sitting in deckchairs on the ground floor, the upper floor was divided into male and female changing areas with a sun terrace on the roof.

Of course, there was a darker tone to the new lifestyle aesthetic. Italian and German beach facilities of the 1930s also featured synchronised swimming

The beach was marketed for the first time as a children's paradise in the 1930s. (Bournemouth Tourism, 1935)

An impromptu performance by the Pierrots in front of a crowded beach, July 1919. Catlin's Royal Pierrots featured a troupe of all-round entertainers like Mr Fred Ellis; a chorus vocalist, dancer, comedian, chapeaugraphist, paper manipulator and lightening oil-painter! (*Bournemouth Graphic*)

Above: Sun worship and bathing
from Bournemouth Pier in 1935.
(Bournemouth Tourism)

Left: Sun worshippers relax on the beach
in 1938; the Council's Tourism department
use the language of Hollywood to sell its
sun-kissed shores. (Bournemouth Tourism)

Bournemouth Pier Approach in 1938, showing the Pavilion and Pier Approach Baths as well as the Bournemouth Club to the west of the pier. (Leisure Services)

displays, athletic trials and communal beach facilities. These were all part of a state programme to toughen up their people for the tasks ahead. And a rather alarming link between fascism and sun worship can be found in a photograph taken at Alum Chine in 1933 in which the *Bournemouth Weekly Post* witnessed 'some happy holiday-makers on August Bank Holiday who signified their pleasure and high spirits with an impromptu march past, Fascist style, one of their number "taking the salute".' Perhaps holidaymakers were simply carried away with the moment, at a time when the Fascists were on a major charm offensive in Britain.

Euphoria and optimism for the future was certainly in the air. Even the much beleaguered pier master at Boscombe was hopeful for the fate of his pier. Robert Lever, the pier master, recalled the following war-time story in an interview published in *The Times* newspaper in 1927.

He told of a sick Egyptian princess visiting Boscombe during the First World War. One of her servants approached Mr Lever to ask for permission to cast some

Solving the bathing problem. By the 1920s, relaxed attitudes to bathing led to people getting changed in their cars rather than hiring the old cumbersome bathing machines. (Drawing by Eustace Nash, by kind permission of his family)

A demonstration of heath and fitness exercises on the beach west of Bournemouth Pier, 1938. (Bournemouth Tourism)

A children's race on the beach, at the start of the 1933 Bournemouth Regatta. (*Bournemouth Weekly Post*)

An alarming and uncomfortable view of holidaymakers on the beach at Alum Chine in 1933. Britain's dalliance with fascism in the early 1930s is often forgotten. (*Bournemouth Weekly Post*)

Characters on the beach were sketched each week for the *Bournemouth Graphic* by local artist Eustace Nash in July 1919. (*Bournemouth Graphic*; reproduced by kind permission of the artist's family)

evil charms into the sea. Her mistress supposed that she would recover her health if the charms were thrown away. The charms were alleged to be ancient Egyptian treasures taken from mummy caskets. At 5 p.m. one afternoon the servant and the princess arrived with the charms and solemnly threw them off the end of the pier. 'We never found out if the Princess recovered, but from that day a new interest was taken in the pier. All the old pessimism seemed to go and people started talking about what we should do with the pier after the war.'

Certainly something had to be done. W. Gordon Wild, proprietor of Keynotes Productions ran concert parties on Boscombe Pier after the war. In September 1920 he complained in a letter to the council that he was closing following heavy losses of £338 that year. This was due to lack of lighting and the poor canvas tent cover over the end of the pier which let in most of the rain. 'I have lost five artistes during the season owing to the entire lack of shelter on the band-stage'. And with a final fit of pique he added, 'services now held near Boscombe Pier entrance by the Salvation Army and the Mission during concerts are distracting the audience and artistes!'

By 1921 the landing stages were ruinous and 'must be removed and replaced,' according to a council report. 'This pier may have been suitable for the times and requirements of 35 years ago, but it is entirely unsuitable for the present day.' The council dithered over replacing the landing stages but matters were settled by a

Boscombe Pier in the 1930s. Notice the canvas roof of the Quarter Deck theatre unfurled on the end of the pier. (Leisure Services)

Boscombe Promenade east of the pier was formally opened by the Prince of Wales on 19 October 1927. (Leisure Services)

flurry of correspondence from the boat operators. The Southampton, Isle of Wight & South of England Royal Mail Steam Packet Co. Ltd gave a typical assessment of the future:

> Having regard to the dangerous approach at certain states of the tide, and the delays arising when disembarking and embarking the very small numbers of passengers in pre-war days as compared with the results of traffic last year when the steamers worked from Bournemouth and Swanage direct, I am strongly of the opinion that Boscombe Pier is of little advantage to us.

Cosens, operators of the *Monarch*, cited the efficient tramway service between Bournemouth and Boscombe as a reason for poor customer demand for their service. The age of steamers at Boscombe Pier had come to an end.

In 1924 the end of the pier was entirely reconstructed in reinforced concrete to take the weight of a concert-hall enclosure surrounded by shelters, a stage and 'Quarter Deck' refreshment rooms. The pier was redecked in Australian Jarrah tropical hardwood, the previously used Scandinavian Pitch Pine having been cut down to commercial extinction by the demands of the First World War. The new

The mayor and his wife join 250 party-goers as the Richards Dance Band play the Quarterdeck Ball on occasion of the reopening of Boscombe Pier in 1927.

pier extension was opened on 29 May 1927 with a glittering ball. Six hundred and fifty guests danced to tunes from Dan Godfrey's Municipal Orchestra. The Mayor, H.J. Thwaites remarked with satisfaction, 'it is now hoped that the pier will pay its way.' This was a sentiment that has not infrequently been expressed by all concerned with the operation of piers for over 100 years!

The new concert arena was open to the skies with a canvas roof for bad weather and featured trumpet amplifiers designed to carry the music played on the pier across the beach either side. The party mood continued through the summer, even when the weather was bad. 'At 10am there was a wild scene at Boscombe Pier head with rain falling and the wind blowing. The crowd soon arrived in gaily coloured costumes covering in coats and macs,' reported the *Bournemouth Times*. The pier itself was illuminated with coloured fairy lights at night.

The new Overstrand Buffet de Luxe had been opened the previous year on the site of the present-day Neptune pub, to feed the revelling crowds. The café featured the most up-to-date kitchen including an automatic dishwasher able to deal with 8,000 pieces of crockery per hour. According to the newspapers, 'exceptional interest [was] shown in the washing-up machine.'

BOSCOMBE PIER

TWICE DAILY ▬ at 3 and 8

— IN —

**SONG
DANCE
OPERA
JAZZ
HUMOUR**

AND

PLAY

W. H. LESTER'S

'Good Companions'

(Titled by special permission of J. B.
Priestley, Esq., Author of the famous
Novel and Play)

Ten Brilliant Artistes

Managers and Leading Critics
unanimous in declaring this to be
the finest and most beautifully
Dressed Show of its kind in the
country.

Advertisement for a performance
on Boscombe Pier, June 1931.
(*Bournemouth Graphic*)

Giant draughts was popular on both piers right up to the 1980s. Here we see Bournemouth Pier in the 1930s. (Leisure Services)

A game of quoits on Bournemouth Pier in the 1930s. (Leisure Services)

Bournemouth Pier Café and solarium, early 1930s. (Leisure Services)

Bands, entertainments and concert parties continued into the 1930s with evergreen shows like 'Good Companions' returning year after year. 'Managers and leading critics are unanimous in declaring,' according to a poster for W.H. Lester's show, 'this to be the finest and most beautifully dressed of its kind in the country.' The show featured Miss Leslie Elliott, the clever comedienne and composer, on the piano; Gerald Farrar and his Rhythm Boys; the alluring Ann Renova; and Ivy Luck bringing the house down with laughter. The sketch revue show 'Bubbles' took over towards the end of the 1930s until war brought an end to the fun.

Bournemouth Pier likewise needed a major overhaul by 1920. In 1916 the magnificent Victorian Gothic pier-entrance building was described in an official report as being in a 'ruinous condition . . . without repairs it is most probable the buildings would have collapsed.' And by 1921, 'it cannot be hoped to make it watertight.' Stormy weather caused considerable vibration in the iron and glass structure. 'This vibration accounts for the broken glass.' The building was finally knocked down and replaced in 1930.

As with Boscombe, Bournemouth Pier also featured a stage and dressing rooms which were added in 1931. A range of popular song and dance shows took place throughout the 1930s. And a solarium was added in 1934.

The seafront continued to prosper throughout the 1930s with deckchairs generating £10,279, cafés £52,500 and bungalows and tents £16,752.

With the onset of war in 1939 the beach amenities initially continued to run as before, but on a much reduced basis. The Army Catering Corps took over the council's East Beach Café in 1940 to service personnel running the army's postal

Crowds of people wait their turn to board the ever-popular steamers, Bournemouth Pier, May 1920. (*Bournemouth Graphic*)

Beach characters from the satirical pen of Eustace Nash, May 1920. (*Bournemouth Graphic*; reproduced by kind permission of the artist's family)

service. There were no longer regular band performances on the piers although a local military band did play occasionally when other duties permitted. Wounded soldiers were permitted free use of deckchairs and free admission to the pier.

Much of the ornate cast-iron seating and lamp columns along the seafront were removed in early 1940 by the Bournemouth Salvage Committee to be used in the production of munitions. And as 1940 wore on, the threat of German invasion became a real possibility. Local military authorities under the command of Major Osborne decided to close access to the seafront in July. Among the mass of barbed wire and anti-tank obstacles laid out across the beach were pipe mines at the bases of the Chines.

The last band performance on Bournemouth Pier took place on the 3 July 1940, as did the final performance of 'Come to the Show' on Boscombe Pier. The very next day all structures above deck level on both piers were ordered to be removed and salvaged for the war effort where possible. Major Osborne then ordered the military to blow up the last three spans of pier neck on Boscombe and Bournemouth Piers to prevent any enemy landing ships from taking advantage of the piers. Formal prohibition of the general public accessing the coastline was announced on 19 August 1940.

The military established blockhouses across the seafront and machine-gun posts in the pier-entrance buildings. Mr N. Ward recalled life as a sixteen-year-old member of the Home Guard, stationed in the clock tower above the entrance building to Bournemouth Pier. Every Sunday he would keep watch out to sea two hours on, two hours off. Sometimes he would be stationed on the sands, below the East Cliff Café.

On 13 January 1945, with the war coming to a close, the seafront was handed back to the council. Work had to begin quickly to clear away all the military installations and make the beach safe in time for summer and the hoped-for return of holidaymakers.

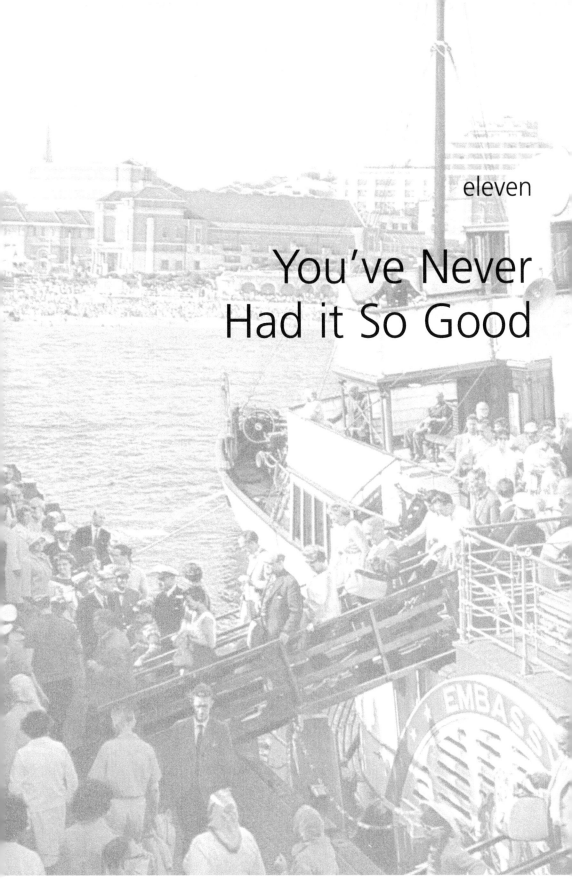

eleven

You've Never Had it So Good

The beach took two years to clear of barbed wire, iron trellis or anti-tank defences, concrete barriers and fallen cliff rubble. Walls had to be repaired and damaged beach offices, cliff lifts, toilets, cafés and bungalows fixed up.

By 1947 the council was flush with proposals to improve the seafront with additional cliff lifts, shelters, bathing stations, new cafés, jetties for pleasure boats and the reinstatement of both piers. However, ambitious plans had to be put on hold as the council grappled with six years of wartime neglect. Large sums were needed to repair the sea wall; new groynes were required as well as new cliff zig-zags at Middle and Durley Chines, Toft Steps, and Southbourne.

Efforts were made to make Bournemouth Pier accessible for pleasure steamers in time for the 1946 season. The temporary gantries connecting the landing stages with the beach were replaced with a full restoration of the pier structure in 1951/52 paid for by war compensation from the government.

Boscombe Pier's future on the other hand, looked bleak. Alderman Little, chairman of the council's Beach and Pavilion Committee, argued that piers 'are really redundant.' The council appealed to the government for funds to pull down it down and were told to do what they liked – but at their own expense. They continued to press for war damage compensation with the proviso that any money received would be spent on new beach facilities, not on repairing the pier. Councillor Benwell responded, 'I disagree that piers are a thing of the past, and the townspeople disagree. It is time someone who believes in piers had the chance to get a move on.' And in 1955, ten years after the end of the war, the council was finally offered compensation by the Ministry of Housing and Local Government to rebuild the pier.

Councillor Benwell was a happy man and told the press, 'a seaside without a pier is like a pig without ears!'

Plans for the complete redevelopment of Boscombe Beach were drawn up. The car park was extended into Honeycombe Chine, a new Overstrand Café and Neptune Bar was built to the east of the pier and a long 450ft shelter was created with over eighty beach huts ranged over two tiers.

The government provided £92,000 and the local council borrowed a further £18,224 to be paid back over thirty years for reconstruction of the pier. Eighteen years of abandonment had left the remaining pier structure in a poor state. The concrete pier head was repairable but the cast-iron work on the neck needed complete replacement. The new pier entrance, concrete neck

A diver prepares to inspect Bournemouth Pier during reconstruction in 1951. (Leisure Services)

Bournemouth Pier in April 1946. The council was anxious to offer steamer services straight after the war, even though the pier itself was far from usable. (Leisure Services)

The entrance building to Boscombe Pier in December 1957 prior to demolition. It was constructed in 1904. (Leisure Services)

COUNTY BOROUGH of BOURNEMOUTH - BOSCOMBE OVERSTRAND CAFE

Architects sketch for the Boscombe Overstrand Café and Neptune Bar, early 1950s. This has been much modified into the Neptune pub today. (Leisure Services)

Boscombe Beach and Overstrand building, east of the pier in 1968. In 2008 the Overstrand building is being remodelled to service the planned artificial surf reef. (Bournemouth Tourism)

and Mermaid pier-head concert hall were designed in-house by John Burton, the borough architect and constructed between 1958 and 1962 by Messrs A. Jackaman & Son Ltd.

The Mermaid Hall on the end of the pier was originally designed to seat 564 people in the expectation that the pre-war concert parties would return. But times had changed and the design was altered to create a multi-purpose hall with a refreshment kiosk at the rear. When the pier reopened on 6 June 1962, the Mayor inaugurated a roller skating rink in the Mermaid Hall with a rather haphazard skate, helpers supporting him on each side. The Mermaid became a favourite meeting place for a whole generation of young people and offered 'modern twist dancing' to the sounds of the 'Sands Combo' for 6s. The Top 20 hits of the day would also be broadcast through

Above: The flying wing Boscombe Pier entrance building takes shape, February 1960. (Leisure Services)

Left: Construction of the cast concrete Boscombe Pier neck underway in February 1959. (Leisure Services)

Roller skating in the Mermaid Hall, Boscombe Pier, soon after opening in 1962. (Bournemouth Libraries)

Boscombe Pier entrance as completed in 1962. Two further retail kiosks were added in 1964. The building was Grade II Listed in 2005. (Leisure Services)

Durley Chine beach looking towards Bournemouth Pier, *c.* 1967. Pedalos and boats are still available to hire today. (Bournemouth Tourism)

a new hi-fi system. Local resident Pat Roe remembers skating to the latest records:

> 'We girls would all have a crush on the older boys who purposely practiced their fancy footwork in front of us – Wilf and Johnny, you know who you are!' In its first year over 97,700 people went on the pier and G. R. Anstee the editor of the Bournemouth Hoteliers' Magazine wrote, 'at last, Boscombe – so long the Cinderella of the area – has something that Bournemouth cannot offer.'

But after only two years the roller-skating craze had faded and despite a great deal of opposition, the building was converted to an amusement hall by Cleethorpes Amusements. Open every day between 10 a.m. and 11 p.m., the renamed 'Palace of Fun' featured bingo, ten-pin bowling, a rifle range and slot machines. A particular favourite was the 'haunted house'. Children would spend all day putting a penny in and wait with great excitement for the 'ghost' to pop up out of the box.

The beach east from Bournemouth pier in August 1966. Compare how this scene has changed from the photograph on page 19, taken from the same angle in 1865. (Leisure Services)

The pier was presided over by retired naval officer Lt.-Cmdr J.W. Perrott who had a small office at the pier entrance.

Boat rides also returned to Boscombe Pier in 1967. John Cutler and his brother Maurice converted a 60ft torpedo recovery boat and set up the Taurus Yacht passenger boat service which ran up until 1975. The *Island Queen* could carry 100 passengers on day trips to Swanage and Yarmouth on the Isle of Wight. They also revived a boat link to Bournemouth Pier with a small open launch called *Sapphire.*

The post-war period for Bournemouth were the real boom years as millions of ordinary people found themselves with greater leisure time and money to spend from the late fifties onwards. At its height, around 40,000 deckchairs were out on the sands. Visitor numbers increased year on year; for instance during August bank holiday weekend in 1957, deckchair takings totalled £2,771 up from £1,736 the previous year. Television showed shots of people sleeping in their cars despite

Bournemouth Pier entrance building, built in 1930, photographed in 1967. The top variety entertainers of the day performed at the Pier Theatre in the 1960s. (Leisure Services)

The Pier Theatre booking office, June 1964. (Leisure Services)

Alum Chine in 1935. The tropical gardens have been freshly laid out on the cliff side. The building at the base of the cliff in the centre of the picture was a boat house, built in 1912, and is now the site of a children's playground. (Bournemouth Tourism)

appeals in the newspapers for more accommodation. Hotels were crowded with 80,000 staying guests and theatres all reported full houses.

In 1959 it was decided to build the present pier theatre, café and bar on Bournemouth Pier. The pier head had to be reinforced with a new concrete base to take the weight of the new 900-seat theatre. The theatre kicked off its first season in 1960 with three performances a day. A children's show in the morning would be followed by comedy and revue in the afternoon. And topping the bill in the evening was Ted Rogers in *Carry on Laughing.* Many household names appeared at the pier theatre over the years such as Arthur Askey, Sid James and Freddie Frinton. By the early eighties television comedy stars would be performing, like the cast of *It Ain't Half Hot Mum, Last of the Summer Wine* and *Hi De Hi.*

Elsewhere along the seafront the council finally purchased the Southbourne section from Mr A. Bedford in 1954, regrading the cliffs to stabilise them and

Above: The Aquabelles synchronised swimming troupe outside the Pier Approach Baths in 1963. (*Bournemouth Guide*)

Left: The *Embassy* steamer in 1965. Pleasure steamers regularly sailed from Bournemouth pier right up to the 1960s. (Bournemouth Tourism)

demolish a number of cliff-top properties in the process. A new sea wall and promenade was also built.

Little Durley Chine, which had contained a pitch-and-putt course before the war, was turned into a yard depot for the corporation.

Alum Chine, having been landscaped once with the creation of the tropical gardens in the 1920s was reworked again in 1955 to create a car park and bus turning circle. The old tennis courts on the cliff top by Alumhurst Road were lost in a cliff slip in 1960 and a children's paddling pool was later installed at the base. The final section of sea wall and promenade was built west of Alum Chine to the Poole boundary in 1955 at a cost of £97,293.

Overall, though, there were no significant changes. The seafront carried on doing what it thought it was best at. The cafés and restaurants were all run by the council and all offered the same fare and the holidaymakers kept on coming. 1976 is reckoned by many to have been the last great year before everyone suddenly discovered cheap package holidays to Spain. From then on, visitor numbers started to decline. The seafront suddenly looked old, tired and in desperate need of reinvestment.

Pier Approach Swimming Baths advertisement, 1965. (Bournemouth Tourism)

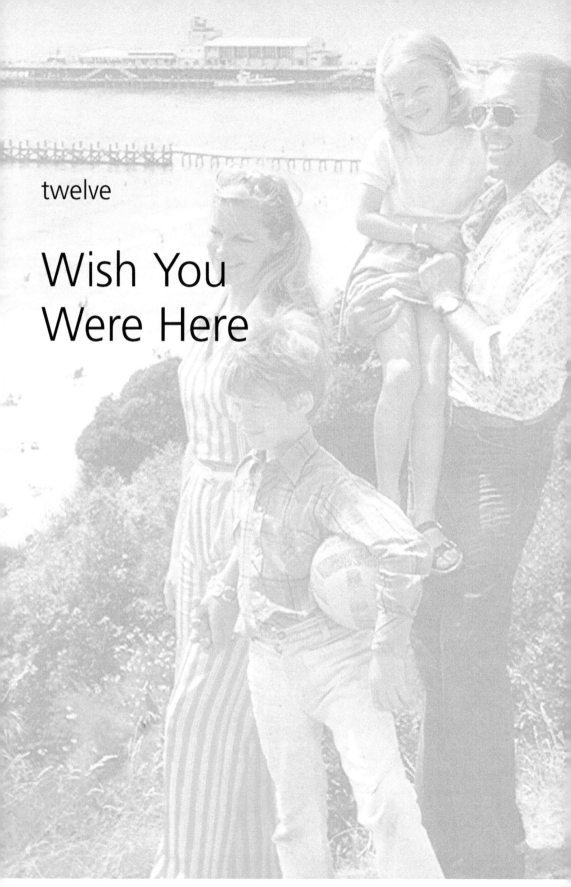

twelve

Wish You
Were Here

Until fairly recently there was an accepted wisdom that the British seaside would never recover. People's expectations had changed markedly. They wanted 'real' holidays abroad that seemingly offered better value for money and guaranteed sunny weather all of the time. The British seaside was too familiar and reminded them of all the shortcomings of home. They wanted new sights and smells. Bournemouth, in common with every resort, saw a heavy decline in the numbers of staying visitors through the 1980s and 1990s and an increasing proportion of day visitors to the beach which was perceived to be a cheap day out.

Insulated slightly by a diverse local economy, Bournemouth did not slip into terminal decline. Plans were laid to reverse the decline by rebuilding Bournemouth Pier at a time when most of Britain's aging Victorian piers were being closed or crumbling into the sea.

Eugenius Birch's iron pier had reached the end of its useful life and a design to rebuild the pier in concrete was drawn up in 1978. In 1979 and 1980 the work was carried out for a sum of nearly £2 million. The old pier-entrance building was also replaced with a new pier leisure centre featuring the Showbar nightclub which became a popular venue in the 1980s and 90s, and an amusement arcade on the ground floor, with shop units around the outside. The clock tower from the old pier-entrance building can now be seen gracing the roof of the James Fisher Medical Centre in the Muscliff area of Bournemouth.

The council had also been assiduously replenishing the beach every ten years or so since the early 1970s to protect the coast against erosion, making the sands much wider than they had been in decades.

The 1980s saw a raft of outside pressures ranging from skin cancer campaigns to groups like 'Surfers against Sewage' and demands to remove sewage outlets. From 1990 onwards, Bournemouth was able to claim Blue Flag status for many of its beaches where the water quality had been cleaned sufficiently to meet high European standards.

Gradually, the old council-run cafés and tea rooms along the front were leased out to private operators with capital to invest and provide the high quality visitors were increasingly demanding. On the down side, litter became an increasing and unsightly problem as people consumed more on the go. By 2007 over 480 tonnes of litter was being removed off the beach and from the bins every year. Community groups supported by the Marine Conservation Society ran volunteer litter picks on the beach to record and highlight the growing

Above: Deck games on Bournemouth Pier in 1967. (Bournemouth Tourism)

Left: Front cover for the *Bournemouth Guide* for 1976. This was probably the last year of the post-war 'golden age' of the seaside holiday. (Bournemouth Tourism)

Opposite above: Fishing off Bournemouth Pier landing stages, 1937. (Leisure Services)

Opposite below: Bournemouth Pier under reconstruction, February 1981. A temporary gangway allows access to the boats and pier theatre. Hotels in the foreground are being demolished to make way for the Bournemouth International Centre. (Leisure Services)

Before the days of clean bathing water, raw sewage used to be pumped out into the bay. This unlucky diver has been tasked with inspecting the sewage pipe which extended beneath Bournemouth Pier, September 1904. (*Bournemouth Graphic*)

problem of litter dumped in the sea and on the beach and its effects on the marine ecology.

The thrust of these campaigns was to right the balance between over-development and natural preservation. An attempt was being made to restore the view and regain the sensory experience enjoyed by the first visitors to Bournemouth's coast over a 150 years before.

New attractions were also built from the late 1990s onwards to lure visitors back. Some were successful, like the Oceanarium, others like the IMAX Waterfront building, built on the site of the Pier Approach Baths, less so.

Increasing beach safety was another area for investment. The KidZone children's beach safety wristband scheme was devised by a Bournemouth schoolgirl in 1996 and has gone on to be adapted around the country, and incidents of lost children on the beach dropped dramatically. CCTV security cameras were also installed in the 1980s and in 2002 the RNLI took on beach life guarding alongside the three volunteer Lifeguard Corps.

By the early twenty-first century, visitor numbers to the beach had stabilised at around four and a half million a year.

Perhaps the most dramatic development in recent years has been a scheme for the wholesale regeneration of the beach down at Boscombe with, at its heart, the most innovative seaside attraction in the UK: Europe's first artificial surfing reef.

The growth in extreme sports such as surfing is all part of a general pull towards experiencing raw and primal thrills that much of modern life insulates against. Once again, the awe and majesty of the sea is drawing visitors as it did at the start of the nineteenth century.

Bournemouth's surfing history goes back to the roots of the UK scene when local pioneer Bob Groves began surfing on his own homemade boards in the early 1960s. He was followed by Roger Castle who helped introduce surfing to a whole generation through the Wessex Surf Club and one of the country's first surf magazines *Tube News*.

The proposal for an artificial surf reef suggested by local resident David Weight in the mid-1990s was eventually incorporated into the wider Boscombe Spa Village regeneration scheme.

Boscombe seafront had been in serious decline since the seventies. The Mermaid Hall on the end of the pier had to be closed in 1990 as the pier-head structure became unsafe. The rest of the pier closed in 2005 for the same reason. Meanwhile, the Overstrand complex of beach huts had also lain largely derelict since the 1990s. Various schemes to revive the area were devised over the years but all fell through due to lack of funding. One proposal called for the creation of a yachting marina built around the pier, but this was considered unfeasible.

Finally, in 2005 the go ahead was secured for the present scheme, funded from the sale of part of the Honeycombe Chine car park for a development of 169 luxury apartments to be called Honeycombe Beach.

In 2007 work commenced on refurbishing the pier and removing the dangerous pier head. The entrance building with its distinctive 'flying wing' roofline was designated as a Grade II Listed structure and has been preserved on the outside whilst opening up the internals to provide new catering and retail facilities. The pier is certainly distinctive and may possibly be the finest example of a twentieth-century modernist pier in the country.

Bournemouth Pier Leisure Centre in 1991. Built in the style of a circus big top in 1981, it housed a popular nightclub called the Showbar until 2006 when it was redeveloped as a restaurant. (Bournemouth Tourism)

Boscombe Pier in the 1980s with the Mermaid Hall on the end of the pier, dismantled in 2007. (Simon Adamson)

Glida boats, Honeycombe Chine, 1930. The boating pond was removed in 1933 and the Chine was filled in and developed into a car park in 1958. Today the site is home to the Honeycombe Beach apartment complex. (Leisure Services)

Boscombe has a tradition for inventing seaside architecture as the San Remo Towers on the hill above amply demonstrates. Built between 1935 and 1938 by American architect Hector Hamilton, it is the best example in this country of the Hacienda style of seaside architecture developed in 1930s Florida.

Most recently, internationally acclaimed HemingwayDesign have been recruited to turn the derelict Overstrand building beach huts, built in 1958, into luxury 'Surf Pods' with bespoke interior designs. The rest of the building is to feature a glass-fronted restaurant, surf hire and retail, public showers and changing facilities. The area in front of the pier is also to be re-landscaped to create a pedestrian space.

The reef itself is to be made of large geo-textile sand bags placed on the seabed over 225m from the shoreline and covering an area the size of a football pitch. Built primarily for enhancing the natural surf with minimal impact on the natural environment, many hope it will also encourage marine diversity and provide some measure of protection against coastal erosion. All eyes will be on Boscombe in the future to see how well the reef performs. But there's no doubt that the economic regeneration effects are already having a positive benefit for the whole Boscombe area.

thirteen

The Future

Children playing in the surf, Bournemouth Beach, 1958. (Bournemouth Tourism)

So what does the future hold for Bournemouth's seafront? Climate change and predicted sea level rises will have a profound effect in the long term. The promenades and sea walls will have to be raised.

Predictions in the growth of eco-tourism present great opportunities to rebrand and lure a new market of ethical visitors. The seafront has made a start through reducing energy wastage, introducing public recycling and becoming the first seaside in the UK to secure a *Green Tourism* award.

A continual programme of reinvestment in facilities with the private sector will be essential. Visions for the future refurbishment of Bournemouth Pier Approach and town centre are already underway.

A drive towards reducing the seasonality of boom and bust is also desired. Schemes like Boscombe Spa Village are intended to create a year-round demand for facilities, with watersports enthusiasts in the winter and traditional beach visitors in the summer.

Calls for greater value for money and a return to the cheap day out to the seaside must also be heeded, as the council seeks to drive up the quality of facilities on offer in partnership with private operators.

Health tourism may yet see a revival in the future. Many new seaside health resorts have been built in recent years in France and on the coast of the Black Sea. And so the story returns full circle to the original aims and ambitions for Bournemouth set out over a century and a half ago.

Bibliography

A Guide to Bournemouth (Abel Heywood & Son, Manchester, 1886)

An Illustrated Account of Bournemouth (Robinson, Son & Pike, Brighton, 1893)

Ashley, Harry & Hugh, *Bournemouth Centenary 1890-1990* (Bournemouth Borough Council, 1990)

Bailey, W.M., *Lease of Overcliff, Cliffs, Beach and Foreshore: Statement of Negotiations with Sir George Meyrick's Solicitors* (Richmond Hill Press, 1902)

Beale, J.E., *One Hundred and Forty-One Views: Bournemouth and Other Hampshire Views* (J.E. Beale, The Fancy Fair, c. 1910)

Bournemouth Seafront Strategy 2007- 2011 (Leisure Services, Bournemouth Borough)

Bournemouth Corporation, Bournemouth, *Britain's All-Seasons Resort The Official Guide, 1938-39* (Bournemouth Corporation, 1938)

Bournemouth Corporation, *The Official Guide to Bournemouth* (Bournemouth Corporation, 1923)

Borough of Bournemouth, Royal Sanitary Institute Health Congress, Bournemouth 1935 (Borough of Bournemouth, 1935)

Brodie & Winter, *England's Seaside Resorts* (English Heritage, 2007)

Bright's Illustrated Guide to Bournemouth (Bright & Co., Bournemouth, 1897)

Butcher, Cole & Co.'s Bournemouth, *Christchurch and Poole Directory* (Butcher, Cole & Co., London, 1874)

Cox, B., *Paddling Across the Bay: The Story of the Bournemouth, Southampton & Weymouth Paddle Steamers* (Paddle Steamer Preservation Society, Wessex Branch: Bournemouth 1981)

Dolamore, F.P., *Report of the Development of the West Beach* (County Borough of Bournemouth, 1920)

Dolamore, F.P., *Municipal Works in the County Borough of Bournemouth* (Paper presented at the meeting of the Institution of Municipal and County Engineers in Bournemouth, 9th May 1919)

Granville, A.B., *Spas of England and Principal Sea-Bathing Places Volume 2* (Adams & Dart: Bath 1971)

Grey, Fred, *Designing the Seaside: Architecture, Society and Nature* (Reaktion Books Ltd, 2006)

Mate, W., *Bournemouth Illustrated* (W. Mate & Sons, 1887)

Miller, A., *Old Bournemouth, the Story of the Bourne Tregonwell Estate* (Bournemouth Local Studies Publications: Bournemouth 1996)

Official Opening of the Extensions to the Promenade, Alum Chine (County Borough of Bournemouth publication, 1957)

Peters, John, *Bournemouth Then and Now: a Pictorial Past* (Ensign publications, Southampton, 1990)

Pugh, Peter, *The Royal Bath* (Cambridge Business Publishing, 1988)

Council, 2007)

Sydenham's Illustrated, *Historical, and Descriptive Guide to Bournemouth* (Bournemouth, 1887)

Thomson, S., *Health Resorts of Britain; And How to Profit by Them* (Ward & Lock: London, 1860)

Watson, W.D., *Bournemouth Pier History* (Unpublished report, Borough Engineer's Department, 1980)

Wigmore, G.I., *Sea Defences in Bournemouth* (unpublished paper, 1951)

Newspapers:

The Bournemouth Graphic (1901 – 1935)

The Daily Echo (1957 to present)

Letters:

Sundry correspondence held in Bournemouth Borough Council's Leisure & Tourism Services Archives, Southcote Road Depot.

Index

Other local titles published by The History Press

Bournemouth
IAN ANDREWS AND FRANK HENSON

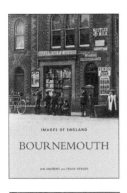

This collection of 200 archive images traces some of the changes and developments that have taken place in the seaside town of Bournemouth during the last century. Pictures include schools and churches, shops and businesses – including Marshall & Bower the builders on Elmes Road and switchboard employees at the G.P.O. Telephone Private Exchange at The Royal Bath Hotel in the 1920s – to sporting events and local townspeople.

0 7524 3065 3

Poole The Second Selection
IAN ANDREWS AND FRANK HENSON

This fascinating collection of over 200 photographs of Poole takes the reader once again on a nostalgic journey through Poole to look at things as they were, not so very long ago. Once familiar buildings, shops and firms can be seen again and Poole people are observed involved in all manner of work and play activities. There is an interesting feature about Poole Town Football Club and another about Poole lifeboats. Schools, hospitals, pubs, churches and carnivals all make an appearance.

978 07524 1024 3

Haunted Poole
JULIE HARWOOD

From heart-stopping accounts of apparitions, manifestations and related supernatural phenomena to first-hand encounters with ghouls and spirits, this collection of stories contains new and well-known spooky tales from in and around Poole. Drawing on historical and contemporary sources Haunted Poole contains a chilling range of ghostly phenemena and is sure to interest anyone with an interest in the town's darker side.

978 07524 4503 8

The South West Coast A Photographic History
CHRIS THUMAN

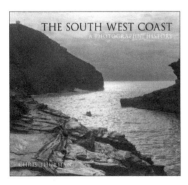

The South West Coast has been a popular holiday destination since Regency days, but the development of the railways and, later, the motor car, brought tourists to the coast in their thousands. The author has photographed the area since boyhood and has captured in these beautiful images the changes that have swept our coastline in the last half century.

978 07524 3961 7

If you are interested in purchasing other books published by The History Press, or in case you have difficulty finding any of our books in your local bookshop, you can also place orders directly through our website

www.the historypress.co.uk